Everybody
on the
Truck!

THE STORY OF THE DILLARDS

---

by LEE GRANT
with the Original Dillards

EGGMAN PUBLISHING

Editor:
  Craig Owensby

Front cover photo:
  Courtesy of Douglas Dillard

Back cover photo:
  Courtesy of *Nashville Now*

Jacket design:
  Michael Walker

Design, typography, and text production:
  TypeByte Graphix (615) 889-2559

Library of Congress: 94-62208

ISBN: 1-886371-11-3

Eggman Publishing
2909 Poston Avenue, Suite 203
Nashville, Tennessee 37203
(800) 396-4626

Dedicated to Jayme, my wife and best friend whose understanding saw me through this project; my daughter and favorite dance partner, Taylor; and to Jack, perhaps the only three-year-old outside the Dillard family to know all the words to "Ebo Walker."

Contents

Acknowledgments

The author expresses his sincere appreciation to all of the individuals who helped put this project together including the folks at *Bluegrass Unlimited*, *Bluegrass Now*, Vanguard Records, Flying Fish Records, Sierra Records, *Nashville Now*, Wildstone Media and Keith Case Management. A tip of the hat is also necessary for Richard Courtney and Kay McGhee at Eggman Publishing for believing in this book from day one.

A special thanks to Denver (Briscoe Darling) Pyle, Maggie (Charlene Darling) Peterson Mancuso, John McEuen and Jim Stafford for their help in filling in the gaps and their willingness to share their experiences with the Dillards. Thanks also to Jim Clark, Greg Kelly, Kathleen Hatchett and Maryglenn McCombs, diehard Dillards fans who provided assistance on the front end of this project.

Thanks to Dean, Douglas, Mitch, Rodney and their families for all their thoughtfulness, hospitality, and use of personal photographs. Meeting the original Dillards was equivalent, for this writer anyhow, to meeting the Beatles. Thanks especially to Mitch who taught me wonderful phrases which I try to work into normal conversation whenever possible such as, "Slicker than deer guts on a door knob," "That dog won't hunt" and of course the opposite, "That dog **will** hunt."

Thanks to the management and staff of the Palace Inn in Branson for the kindness and the friendliness shown to this road-weary traveler, and for providing excellent tips on food and directions.

Finally thanks to the Dillards as a group, who brought a little more fun and good music into this world.

Everybody On The Truck!

A Word From Denver Pyle

Paws are undeniably partial when it comes to talkin' about their own, but the Dillards (I don't know why they had to go and invent one of them pseudo names) were nice fellas blessed with a natural gift of music.

Nothing tickled me more than performing with the boys and their pretty adopted sister, Maggie Peterson, on *The Andy Griffith Show*. When Mitch Jayne, Dean Webb, Rodney and Douglas Dillard shuffled out of their dressing room for the first time in their going to town duds, I realized at first glance that they were the spittin' image of what the script writers must have envisioned.

Folks ask me why the writers refused to let the boys talk. Well, when you throw four lanky boys together on a teeny-tiny stage, already crowded with cameras, lights, props, musical instruments and all those other contraptions, before you know it a lot of voices start cluttering up the works. Silence, a great man once remarked, is golden, and the boys' characters were pure fourteen carat. Besides, a reasonable man could judge right away just by studying the boys' faces that they were too plain excited to speak.

The question most often asked by fans is to name a favorite episode or scene from *The Andy Griffith Show*. Honestly, after so many years the shows all tend to run together. I reckon *Mountain Wedding* holds the dearest place in my heart. That picture of the whole Darling family snoring in five-part harmony is a pure gut buster. Here's the story behind the story for you to ponder. Briscoe and the boys are asleep in their cabin the night before Charlene is to marry Dud Wash. Dean, the mandolin-playing member of the family, started to snore, then Rodney picked it up with the alto part. Within minutes the boys are all snoring in a beautiful four-part harmony, and I come in with the bass snore. Next thing I heard was this huge guffaw from Andy, and then a loud crash as he fell from his chair and hit the floor with a resounding bang. He just couldn't hold it in anymore. Don Knotts followed quickly and within a matter of seconds the entire set had deteriorated into riotous laughter, infecting every member of the cast and crew. The scene was the first shot of the day and it took us to lunch to film it without someone breaking down.

Certain phrases still catch me off guard. I'll be in the marketplace picking over some taters or beans and a stranger will recognize me, stare me in the eye, grin and shout, "Slack off! Slack off!" or "Your kisses are to be treasured, but they just ain't worth the pain." These expressions have become passwords to fans of the Darlings.

People ask where Briscoe came from. He is really a compilation of a lot of people. There's a smidgen of

The Dillards as they appeared on *The Andy Griffith Show* as the Darlings. (l-r) Andy Griffith, Douglas Dillard, Dean Webb, Rodney Dillard and Mitch Jayne along with co-star Denver Pyle. —*photo courtesy of the Dillards*

Walter Brennan in Briscoe, mixed in with dabs of just about every other old codger that I'd met along the way.

Folks wonder why I took such a shine to those Missouri boys, but the pure gospel is that talent is talent and those boys were fine bluegrass musicians. Truth be told, I'd been a bluegrass fan long before most people started collecting that type of music. I admired those great bluegrass performers like Bill Monroe and the others you would see on *Nashville Barn Dance*. They played wonderful songs that touched your heart, like "Wreck on the Highway" (that one still makes me cry) and all those other great standards. I started collecting those classic bluegrass tunes in the early 50s, never imagining that I'd one day share the stage alongside a bluegrass band as gifted as the Dillards.

I should add here that my fondness for music sprang up honestly. My mom and dad played guitar and fiddle at dances in eastern Colorado for ages. My grandpa was an amazing fiddle player even though he got his hand crushed underneath a rocking chair when he was a little baby.

Ours was a dirt poor family. Sure, there were cars and trains carrying folks here and yonder, but not at our house. My mom and dad traveled by horse and wagon to play at barn dances. If they'd been hired on for a dance on Saturday night, they might've had to head out early Friday in order to get there sometime Saturday afternoon. They would play all night and then load up the wagon and drive them horses back home and maybe not reach the house till Monday. All this travel and work might have earned them four dollars, which to them was a lot of money.

When she wasn't singing or playing for a paying audience, mother would practice on the children. Ma would gather all us youngsters around close and serenade us with those old sad songs like "Mother is in Heaven," and we would just start blubbering.

The Dillards shared similar humble backgrounds, which I think added reality to the characters. There was a sincerity about the Darling family that immediately struck a chord with the American television audience. There was a warmth about the family that audiences could relate to back then, and still do to this day.

I suppose here is as good a place as any to make my confession. Although I've always had a passion for music, I've never had what they call a musical ear. I made some noises with those jugs, but after the musical numbers were shot a fella would come in to play water bottles which had been tuned. This water bottle music would then be dubbed in over my jugging. Of course, when the Darlings reunited for appearances on *Nashville Now*, or occasional concerts like one in Dodge City for the American Medical Association, I would play the jug. I never understood why, but there always seemed to be one bass player standing way back in the wings, peering at me and trying to keep up with me. He explained to me once that he was trying to improve my juggin', but I told him I'd never got any complaints.

A fact scant people know is that the boys contributed more to *The Andy Griffith Show* than simply musical interludes. Dean, for instance, was a fine researcher. He was the one who found the perfect song for Briscoe to sing while courting Aunt Bee. "Low and Lonely," a Roy Acuff tune, was the first song I'd ever sang on television, and let me tell you, I was as nervous as the proverbial long-tail cat in a room full of rocking chairs. I'd sing a line in one key and another line in a different key. By the time we finished filming that scene I had managed to collect a whole ring of keys. But through the magic of editing they pieced the song together, and the final version sounded pretty good.

The Darling family gathers together every once in a blue moon, whenever there is a hoot-owl pie baking in the oven or somebody has a new song to play. The boys have performed with me a couple of times on *Nashville Now* to promote Uncle Jesse's Fishing Tournament for the Special Olympics, held each year in Paris, Texas.

Once, when Rodney was working for Jim Stafford's show in Branson, Missouri I went down to watch Rodney perform. Word reached Stafford that Briscoe Darling was in the audience, and he called me up on stage to play a tune with Rodney. Jim handed me a brand spanking new jug and we jumped right into a rendition of "Dooley." We nearly brought the house down that night. Rodney claimed it looked like the resurrection of Elvis had occurred, but I don't recall Elvis ever playing the jug.

When Andy asked the family to gather round once again for *Return to Mayberry* it was like we had never been apart. Personally, I think the show could have benefited from a few more tunes, but the show was still a lot of fun.

Looking back, one of my regrets is that the Darlings never went on the road for an extended tour. Still, the boys seemed to do themselves proud on their own, and you've got to cut them apron strings at some point.

So there ya have my two cents. The rest of the story is contained in the following pages, so as Briscoe would say, find a place to jump in and hang on tight.

All right—*everybody on the truck!*

—Denver Pyle

The Old Home Place

European music critics credit the Dillards as the founders of country-rock. Yet Dillard music begins neither with Douglas or Rodney Dillard, but with their parents, Homer Earl Dillard and Lorene Dillard. Life inside the Dillard home centered on Homer's fiddle and Lorene's guitar. No family squabbles or bickering ever managed to silence the strumming and picking of instruments. Music represented the touching of the stone which kept the family together through any tragedies or personal hardships.

Rodney and Douglas Dillard credit their musical roots to their father, who in turn had learned from his father before him, John William Dillard. As a child growing up in Burns, Tennessee, Homer Dillard listened in wonder as fiddlers played and danced at barn dances. Before he had a fiddle to call his own, Homer would grab two sticks from a wood box, pretend one was the fiddle and the other the bow, and rub the sticks together trying to keep time with the grown-ups. When he wasn't practicing alone Homer kept a keen eye glued on the musicians, and he tried to memorize every movement and every tune. Not content to master the fiddle, he went a step further by teaching himself how to dance while playing. He did this by telling his mother that he was going out

These three childhood friends later reunited to produce two al-
bums, *Permanent Wave* and *Glitter Grass from the Nashwood
Hollyville Strings*. (l-r) Rodney Dillard, John Hartford and
Douglas Dillard   —*photo courtesy of Flying Fish Records*

to finish his daily chores, then sneaking up into the
hayloft and wearing out pair after pair of shoes
while trying to recollect dance steps.

Years later, when Homer and Lorene's own children came along, he purchased a radio and set up a
forty-foot antenna. The family gathered around the
glow of the three radio dials each night, straining to
hear the latest in country music from a station over
in Jefferson City. Sensing his children's interest in
music, Homer decided to rescue his fiddle from its
premature retirement. Lorene joined in with her guitar, and the first Dillard band was born. While children today gather around the television set in the eve-

nings, the Dillard young came together around Homer Dillard's fiddle.

The couple played and sang songs for the children every night until music became a natural part of the family's daily ritual as natural as eating. When the children sprouted big enough to hold their own instruments, Homer and Lorene began teaching Rodney and Douglas the basics of the fiddle and guitar. By the time he was five years old, Douglas was already adept enough on the fiddle to second for his father and could chord the guitar. As the years of fiddling drifted sweetly along, Homer felt a certain sound was missing. The family band needed a banjo picker, so he scoured the area for a five-string instrument. Finding none available, he ordered Douglas a Kay five-string from the Sears and Roebuck Christmas Wishbook. Homer's wish for a banjo player came true on Christmas morning 1952 when they handed Douglas his first banjo. The first song Douglas learned how to play on the banjo was a two-finger picking rendition of "Green Corn."

Childhood friends of Douglas and Rodney, such as future fiddler/songwriter John Hartford, dropped in frequently to jam with the Dillards. The children would stay up into the wee hours of the night, listening, playing and learning tunes from Homer until they passed out from sheer exhaustion. Homer would then leave for his job as a government meat inspector for the Swift Company. Once his shift was finished he would return, rouse the boys from their sleep, and invite them to play some more.

Homer Dillard's talent and spirit is captured on two biographical videos. *A Night in the Ozarks*, produced by John McEuen, a founding member of the

Nitty Gritty Dirt Band, reveals the elder Dillard's showmanship as he fiddles and dances through the film. The second, *Precious Memories*, produced by Tom Shipley, is a bittersweet portrait of Homer returning with his wife, children and grandchildren on a pilgrimage to the family's ancestral home in Burns. *Precious Memories* begins in Homer and Lorene's Salem, Missouri home, and includes footage of the patriarch playing with Douglas, Rodney and other family members and friends. The video concludes with the trip to Burns and the nearby town of Dickson, where Homer served as grand marshal in the Oldtimers Day Parade. Sadly, at the time the latter video was filmed, Homer Dillard was dying of lung cancer. While he lived long enough to see most of the preliminary prints, the final version was released after his death.

"When he passed away, he grabbed at mom's hand and then sort of waved good-bye," Douglas recalled.

Homer Dillard's melodic legacy continues to flourish and is heard through the musical creations of Douglas and Rodney Dillard.

Banjo in the Hollow

Douglas Dillard

Passion for music, Douglas Dillard contends, was instilled in him from his birth on March 6, 1937. His love of music was evident long before he picked up a fiddle or a banjo. Douglas' introduction to banjo picking came before he learned how to walk: one weekend, his parents drove to Nashville to watch the Grand Ole Opry and Douglas, only a year old, tagged along. The sight of Uncle Dave Macon's spirited banjo picking left an indelible impression on the toddler.

"I can still remember seeing Uncle Dave Macon on stage. Of course, at the time I had no idea what it was he was playing, but I thought it was great. He was so wildly animated that he would do things like throw his banjo up in the air." he recalled.

When Douglas became a proficient picker on his Kay five-string, Homer and Lorene Dillard rewarded him with a Gibson model. Douglas' affection for and inherent skill on the banjo had fulfilled Homer Dillard's desire to have a banjo picker in the family (Rodney played the guitar, while the eldest brother, Homer Earl, Jr. played the accordion and piano). The only fly in the ointment was that Douglas, who never received any formal training on the instrument, didn't realize that banjo players used picks.

"I had no idea how to use a pick properly. The first time I ever used fingerpicks they were old rusty ones, and I put them on backwards. My parents drove me to Nashville one day and the next thing I knew we were knocking on the door of Earl Scruggs' home. Earl didn't know my dad from Adam, but he was one of the kindest and most hospitable men in the world. He invited us inside and gave me a lesson on picking. He even gave me a couple of his own picks," Douglas explained.

Years later, Douglas would repeatedly return the lesson of compassion that Scruggs had taught him. Mitch Jayne relates the story of a young banjo picker who met his idol, Douglas Dillard, backstage after a concert.

"This little kid was probably ten years old, and his father had bought him his first banjo. It was a Kay model, which is the Sears Roebuck of banjos, and most of them sound like they are full of dirty shorts. They have to be worked with, honed down, and tuned, and have the head tightened. You have to adjust the bridge and all of this and that before they ever sound like anything. Douglas sat down with the boy, talked to him about his banjo and made over it like it was about the finest banjo he had looked at in days and days. Douglas told the boy, 'Now, this banjo is like all other musical instruments. It has to belong to you. Once it belongs to you it will have a personality of its own. It won't sound like any other banjo. Let me show you some little tricks you can do with it.' And while he is sitting there talking to that little kid, Douglas is all the while shaving down the bridge, tightening down the head, and moving the bridge up to a better place to suit the kid's short stubby fingers. When he finished, he handed the banjo back to the boy and said, 'Now play something for me.' The kid said he only knew

one song. Douglas shook his head and said, 'Well, I know that song—let me play with you.' It was a children's song out of a little kid's first lesson book, and Douglas started playing harmony behind him. Douglas got way up on the neck and started playing these beautiful, intricate musical doilies around this little kid. It was like watching a piece of absolute magic. Douglas had that kid hypnotized like a bird with a snake. The little kid was being made to feel like an incredible musician because Douglas was playing with him. Since then, I've seen Douglas do that to fiddlers and other banjo players countless times. He made them sound like twice the banjo player that they were, because Douglas was doing all the right things behind him. Not showing off, mind you, but playing backup. Douglas' whole face would light up like a Jack O'lantern with the sheer joy of getting the very best out of the person he was playing with."

Always an avid Earl Scruggs fan, Douglas' emotional attachment to Scruggs' music cost him the use of a 1934 Plymouth. Driving along a country road one afternoon, Douglas was listening to the radio when "Earl's Breakdown" boomed through the speakers. Douglas lost himself in the pure excitement of hearing the song for the first time and drove off into a ditch.

Douglas never imagined that he would actually become a professional musician. Like his brother Rodney, Douglas spent his youth playing for the squirrels, birds and rabbits which occupied the nearby woods or at local pie suppers. Saturday nights were spent performing in a unique traveling music show of sorts. Douglas and his lifelong buddy Bill Glenn would hop into the back seat of a friend's car with their instruments. Douglas, naturally, played the banjo, while Glenn accompanied him on guitar.

A blonde Rodney Dillard (second from left) and Douglas Dillard (banjo) perform on Mitch Jayne's Hickory Hollow Time at KSMO in Salem, Missouri.   —*photo courtesy of Douglas Dillard*

Mutual friends drove the pair up and down the streets of Salem as the teen-age musicians played songs for anyone who would listen.

As their virtuosity increased, Douglas and Rodney, along with Glenn and friends Henry Lewis, Jim Lewis, and Paul Breidenbach, formed the Ozark Mountain Boys. Mitch Jayne, a local radio personality, invited the boys to play on "Hickory Hollow," his weekly Saturday morning radio show on KSMO in Salem. Douglas later penned a banjo tune and named it "Hickory Hollow," as a tribute to Mitch's former program.

"The first time the Ozark Mountain Boys played on KSMO, I thought I was going to faint," Douglas chuckled. "We didn't get paid to play. We just performed for the experience of being on radio, and we liked working with Mitch. When Rodney got a little bit older, he played in the band with us."

Douglas and Rodney later teamed with John Hartford, Buddie Van and Joel Noel to form the Dixie Ramblers. The young musicians were infrequently heard in local clubs around the St. Louis area, but the Dillard brothers soon left the band.

Upon graduating from high school, Douglas enrolled in Washington University at St. Louis, which would later become the site of the Dillards' first professional concert. Upon leaving Washington University, Douglas spent the next few years as a bookkeeper at the Edward D. Jones Company in St. Louis, engulfed by a sea of paper and yearning for adventure. The decision to hit the road came after a telephone call from his younger brother. Calling from a pay phone on the Southern University campus, Rodney moaned that school no longer held any interest for him and that he planned to attempt a career in music. Instead of receiving an argument from his brother to quit talking such nonsense and remain in school, Rodney received an offer for a partnership.

"I was really getting tired of bookkeeping. I could envision myself slaving away behind the same desk for twenty-five years, until they gave me a gold watch and showed me the door," Douglas recalled. "My whole life would have passed me by with nothing much to show for it."

Rodney and Douglas agreed to try their luck in California. Douglas reasoned that even if the brothers failed, he could always snare another job as a bookkeeper.

Back home in Salem, the brothers sharpened their

skills. They performed with a variety of groups, and occasionally drifted to Lake of the Ozarks and sat in at the Ozark Opry. Their first recording deal was not as the Dillards, but as the Dillard Brothers. The pair cut two records, "Banjo In The Hollow" and "You Are On My Mind," on the K-Ark label in St. Louis. Accompanying them on the records were Van and Noel. Douglas' first banjo tune, "Banjo In The Hollow," has become a Dillards' classic. The song title is now used by the Grand Ole Opry Chapter of The Andy Griffith Show Rerun Watchers Club.

Rodney Dillard

Rodney Dillard was born in East St. Louis, Illinois on May 18, 1942, and is five years younger than Douglas. Like his older brother, Rodney's earliest recollections of home life not surprisingly focus on music.

"The first imprinting as a child that hangs in my memory is of my mother playing the guitar and Dad playing the fiddle while people sat around in either the kitchen or living room. Honestly, I can remember laying in a crib and listening to their music. Music was such an everyday part of our lives that I thought every family was the same way."

Lorene was a disciple of reverse psychology. When Douglas and Rodney grew big enough to hold a guitar, she would stick hers behind the sofa and admonish the children to keep their hands off it. Naturally, Douglas and Rodney would snatch the instrument from behind the couch immediately after she left the room and start beating and plucking the strings.

"She was a pretty smart lady. She and Dad always encouraged us to learn how to play instruments. When they thought Douglas and I had learned enough, our parents bought us our own instruments. I think dad just wanted a back-up band for his fiddle," Rodney said. "I remember when Douglas got his first banjo, he took it outside and burned his initials into it with a magnifying glass."

A short while later Rodney received a Silvertone guitar, and when he achieved a greater level of competence, his parents rewarded him with a Martin. Playing with their parents was a joyful experience for the brothers.

"Dad was an old-time fiddle player. Our music sounded like that of the old "Skillet Lickers" and "Fruit Jar Drinkers" (bands which performed on the Grand Ole Opry). As we grew older, Douglas became extremely proficient in the banjo and amazed everyone." the younger Dillard said.

Rodney's musical accomplishments drew similar awe-inspired responses. While still a mere student at William H. Lynch Grammar School, Rodney claimed possession of first chair trumpet on the Salem High School Band. Playing the trumpet provided an early indication of Rodney's diverse musical interest. Neither his father, nor Douglas understood why Rodney would want to play anything other than bluegrass music.

"I had this other musical side of me that wasn't gelling with what Douglas and Pop were doing musically. So many people get locked into one type of music and think that a bluegrass player is only a bluegrass player. Later on in life, as I spent more time in Los Angeles and in the musical world, the more that other side of musical interest began to re-surface," Rodney said.

The Dillard family played at church socials and family get-togethers, but never professionally. The boys' parents were too busy earning a living to pursue music as a career. Their parents both worked in East St. Louis during the week, although the family home was in Salem, Missouri—a good hundred miles away on Route 66, which was just a two-lane road at the time. The boys were raised by their aunt Dollie McNeil during the week, and by their parents on the weekends. Aunt Dollie taught Rodney to read before he reached school age, and transformed him into a voracious reader.

"Our parents were the typical hard-working, middle-class stock, who believed in family values. Mom was a seamstress who worked in the garment district of East St. Louis, although she also sewed at home for others. Dad might have missed one-half of a day in the forty years that he worked at the Swift Company meat packing plant," Rodney explained. "East St. Louis was the big city to us country kids. We would sometimes visit our parents in the city, but we could never get used to all the noise. Even at night there was a roar and we couldn't sleep. But city people complain about the country just for the opposite reason. They can't sleep, because it's too quiet."

Rodney spent the summers of his youth exploring ponds and fishing all day. While he patiently waited for an unsuspecting fish to bite, Rodney entertained himself by composing tunes in his head.

"When we finally got a television I watched these musicians perform, and I remember saying to myself, 'One of these days you're going to be doing this.'

A very young Rodney Dillard (back row, left) joined his brother
Douglas (front row, right) and John Hartford (front row, left) in Joel
Noel's Dixie Ramblers.   —*photo courtesy of Douglas Dillard*

There was no explanation for that thought. I wasn't
hit by a bolt of light, nor did some invisible voice
make some revelation about my musical future. It
was just a feeling that came over me, and at that
point I took a more serious interest in playing the
guitar," he said.

Rodney lugged his guitar with him wherever he
went, playing in parks or in the back seats of cars on
country roads. Meanwhile, Douglas had graduated
from high school and had moved on to Washington
University in St. Louis. Rodney's dream of recording

professionally came true with the production of the
K-Ark and Marlo Records label songs. Cradling that
first vinyl disc tenderly in his hands ranks as one of
Rodney's most cherished memories.

"Our folks were still working in the city and
didn't get home until about midnight or one o'clock
in the morning," Rodney said, smiling as he relived
that moment in time. "We couldn't wait to play that
record for them. Douglas and I played it over and
over and over that night. I don't think I've ever had a
greater thrill in my life than playing that first record."

Not everyone offered encouragement to Rodney.
During his senior year at Salem High School, Rodney
was unexpectedly summoned to the principal's office. He received a double-edged pep talk of sorts.

"He told me, 'Rodney, you have a lot of potential
if you stay focused on your school work. Your scores
are in the upper five-percentile nationally, but you
are plain wasting your time in music. Give it up, because you just won't make anything of yourself in
music.' I looked at him and thought to myself, 'Well,
forget you.'"

From that day forward, Rodney started slacking
off in his daily lessons. Older friends would pick him
up each day at noon, and they would spend their
lunch breaks tooling down the back roads, finding
places to practice their music. Weekends were spent
performing with various bluegrass bands in local
bars. This sometimes proved tricky, as Rodney was
still underage. Occasionally, the club manager or bartender would realize that Rodney wasn't of legal age
and order him to leave. Rodney soon learned the art
of sneaking into clubs by sliding in with a crowd or

having another band member divert the bartender's attention while Rodney quietly ducked inside.

Those early clubs were not even remotely similar to places like The Hungry I, The Mecca, or The Cellar Door where the Dillards would perform before eager audiences years later. Instead, they were tough hangouts where brawls were viewed as part of the nightly entertainment.

"We played in some of the real tough clubs in East St. Louis, where the bars were located under the bridge. These were the clubs where all the displaced second-generation country folk from Arkansas and Southeast Missouri would congregate. They had all migrated to St. Louis chasing the elusive American dream of finding a better job and life. It was like a country ghetto filled with displaced rural persons stuck in an urban situation. They were very much like the Irish immigrants who settled in Boston. They tended to stay in one area, and all of them went to the same corner bar. These were the people we played music with, and were the people who came to hear us play," he recalled.

Rodney reluctantly enrolled as a freshman at Southern University. His plan was to major in psychology, as it was the only subject which held any interest for him. His heart wasn't in book learning and, as the months passed, he realized that he simply didn't belong in college. A few weeks before final exams, Rodney wandered to a telephone booth and called Douglas. He confessed to his lack of interest in college and declared that he was leaving Southern. When Douglas agreed with his decision, Rodney returned to campus, packed his bags, and headed home. He never looked back.

Back in Salem, the boys hooked up with Mitch Jayne and plotted their future. They envisioned themselves performing to standing-room-only audiences in faraway cities such as Los Angeles and San Francisco. Record producers would be lining up to sign them to long-term contracts. Agents would be beating down their Beverly Hills mansion doors, clutching lucrative television and movie contracts in one hand and cash in the other. All they needed was a few good songs, a mandolin player, and a little cash to finance the trip.

Finding the mandolin player was simple. The Dillards called Dean Webb and laid out their plan. Dean eagerly agreed to join the band and drove to Mitch's house, the band's temporary headquarters, in Salem.

Dean Webb

Dean Webb was born March 28, 1937, in Independence, Missouri, the son of Carol Crawford and Clarence Webb. Dean spent his entire childhood in Independence, which perhaps explains his longing to follow the sun.

"My mother was a registered nurse, while my father was a jack of all trades. He ran a couple of filling stations and dabbled a bit in farming. He bought a little farm, actually it was just a small piece of property south of Independence, and we used to go out there and rough it on the weekends. My mother wasn't very crazy about living in the country, but she would go out there with us every now and then."

Growing up in the 1940s, Dean and his brother Gene spent hours listening to singing cowboys over

Bob Crawford (front row, third from left) was a member of The Texas Rangers and a musical inspiration to his nephew, Dean Webb. —*photo courtesy of the Crawford family*

KMBC Radio out of Kansas City, Missouri. Radio stations frequently hired local musicians then to broadcast live on regular programs. KMBC's lineup included the "Dinner Bell Round-up Gang, starring The Texas Rangers." The band featured a quartet of country and western singers backed by four musicians. Bob Crawford, Dean's uncle, was one of the group's singers and songwriters, and it was from Crawford that Dean and Gene developed their interest in music. Gene played cowboy songs on the guitar, but a hand injury prevented him from pursuing a career in music, Dean explained.

"We thought the Texas Rangers were as big, or as

popular as anybody, because they were local favorites," Dean explained. "Western music was very popular then, and my uncle's group was sent to California twice to play in the movies."

Saturday-afternoon westerns were typical matinee attractions throughout the country. The demand for westerns and the popularity of singing cowboys created plenty of opportunities for back-up bands. Westerns that featured singing cowboys such as Gene Autry, Johnny Mack Brown, Tex Ritter and Roy Rogers regularly hired Western bands. The band members always played the parts of the ranch hands who hung around the bunkhouse until Gene or Tex needed to sing a song. Then, out would come the instruments and the ranch hands would transform themselves into a band. The "Texas Rangers" were among these groups of bunkhouse boys.

In later years, Dean learned that he and his uncle had shared similar misfortunes when it came to timing. When the Dillards landed in Los Angeles the sun was already beginning to set on folk music, and though the Dillards' songs were well received by club audiences, they were rarely heard on the radio. Nearly twenty years earlier Crawford had written "There's An Old Rail Fence," which played well on the various national music charts. Record sales lagged, not because of a lack of interest, but due to a shortage of vinyl brought on by World War II.

By the time Dean entered the fourth grade, he was taking piano lessons. He studied classical music for four years, but eventually lost interest in the piano when his teacher fell ill and was replaced by another instructor.

"I never really identified with the piano," Dean

stated matter-of-factly. "When I started listening to bluegrass records of Bill Monroe I found myself identifying more with what Monroe was doing with the mandolin."

When Dean graduated from William Crisman High School in 1955, his musical interest focused on traditional country singers such as Faron Young and Hawkshaw Hawkins. Listening to the radio, Dean started to notice a different sound.

"The station played a few bluegrass tunes on a very infrequent basis. I've always been the type of person that liked things that were scarce, better than if it was popular," he explained.

Dean and two cousins, Duane and Clifford Webb, started experimenting with different instruments. Originally, Dean leaned toward learning either the banjo or the fiddle, but Duane and Clifford had already claimed those and sounded pretty good. He wanted to add a different sound to the group, and considered the guitar. Alas, a friend was already adept on the guitar, so he found himself searching for another instrument. He settled on the mandolin—his fourth choice of instruments, and also took it upon himself to learn the bass.

"When you listen to bluegrass music, it's the banjo that catches your ear first, then the fiddle, and then the regular guitar. The stand-up bass is a fairly easy instrument to play, because you only have to learn about three chords. Just about every bluegrass picker will learn about three different instruments, so you can jam with other pickers and swap instruments around. Well, I wanted to play along with bluegrass bands, but I wanted to play something different. I started buying a lot of bluegrass records by

Bill Monroe and Jethro Burns, and I really started to identify with what Monroe was doing on his records. I bought my first mandolin in 1956, a F5 model which was the same model that Monroe used, and I taught myself how to play," Dean recalled.

The group played for hospitals and retirement homes in Independence and Kansas City on a volunteer basis. The audiences were very receptive to the band's sound, and to the fact that young people were taking the time to cheer them up.

Dean came to the bitter realization, though, that enjoying bluegrass music and earning a living playing bluegrass tunes were two entirely different things. At one period just about every resident of Independence claimed relations to some fiddler or bluegrass picker, but tastes were changing at about the time Dean was venturing into music. Folks seemed almost embarrassed to admit that their father or grandpa played a fiddle, as it lacked sophistication and was considered "hick" music. Bluegrass gigs were as scarce as hens' teeth, but Webb was intent on earning his keep through music. He accepted a job as a bass player in a local band which played dance music in the various honky tonks.

Drifting in and out of various jobs like Ebo Walker trying to keep his belly filled and his whistle wet, Dean always returned to music. Jobs in porcelain plants or ice factories held no appeal for the mandolin picker; he wanted to travel the world while he was young and full of energy.

He eventually hooked up with a young banjo picker, Lonnie Hoppers, and Bob Penny to form a bluegrass band, the Ozark Mountain Boys. (This group was different than Douglas Dillard's band,

Promotional poster of the Ozark Mountain Boys. (l-r) Dean Webb,
Cousin Kelly Edwards, Lonnie Hoppers, Dude Fellers, M.C.,
Len Willie and Jan McGuire with Bashful Bob in front.
—*photo courtesy of Dean Webb*

which used the same name.) Penny (known as Bashful Bob) provided comic relief, as well as playing the
bass and guitar.

"We played anywhere we could find, even if was
just a barbershop. For a while we worked out of an
old theater in Hermitage, Missouri. They would hold
local talent contests once a week, which drew big
crowds. Everybody in town would come to see how
their kids would do on stage. The rent didn't satisfy
the owners, and they soon turned it into a pool hall,"
Dean said.

Jim Walter Homes sponsored the band on the *Jim
Walter Jubilee* television program, which aired on
weekends over KOLR in Springfield. Dean's band
also appeared on a Joplin, Missouri television program. In both instances, the agreement was that the

group would receive air time to perform their songs and promote future gigs, but no money.

Dean had met dozens of bluegrass musicians through the years at various festivals and pie suppers. One day Dale Sled, a member of the legendary Osborne Brothers band, introduced Dean to Rodney and Douglas Dillard. A kinship born by a mutual love of bluegrass was immediately struck, and soon thereafter Dean accepted the Dillards' invitation to join them in St. Louis for a weekend jam session.

"About a year later I got another call from Rodney," Dean said. "He explained that they were considering going to California with Mitch Jayne to try their hand at performing, and wanted me to come along."

Dean had met Mitch a year earlier at a bluegrass festival in Salem. Dean had performed with the Ozark Mountain Boys and Mitch, working for KSMO Radio, had introduced the act. Dean, who repeatedly was said to be "as straight as Dick Tracy," would find himself introduced in many ways by Mitch and Rodney Dillard during the next few years. Rodney often commented to audiences that "Dean is the only man I know who irons his toothpaste tube."

Mitch would refer to Dean as the quiet member of the band; people almost forgot he was there. The problem, Mitch reasoned, was that Dean was plain too thin to be seen by most audiences.

"If Dean stood sideways and stuck out his tongue, he'd look like a zipper," Mitch remarked, drawing a roar of laughter from the audience.

Dean's practical side proved beneficial on numerous occasions, although Douglas might grumble about Dean being too picky at times. Dean accepted the role of the Dillards' official hotel inspector. His job was to check the rooms and determine that they met all the necessary requirements. Did all the windows open properly? Were the beds soft? Did the plumbing work? Was the place clean? Did it offer food service, or at least have a restaurant nearby?

Mitch related the following experience in which the Dillards couldn't argue with Dean's sensibilities.

"Dean would march through the room and check all of these things while the rest of us would sit outside in the van and wait. Sometimes Dean would look at two or three places before he would settle on one. Once, while Dean was checking out a motel, Douglas said to me, 'Why does Dean have to take so long.' I told him that it was just Dean's way, and he replied, 'Well, it don't take me that long to look at a horseshoe,' which is a great Ozark expression that is useful for all kinds of things.

"Well, I watched Dean through the van window as he marched through the motel lobby, flipped the room key onto the reception desk and headed back to the van.

" 'What's the matter with this place?'

" 'Bullet holes in the connecting doors,' Dean answered in that calm voice of his. 'Always a sign of unrest.' "

Mitch Jayne

Mitch Jayne is easily recognized as the bass-playing member of the Dillards. Bass takes on a completely different meaning when discussing bluegrass music. Paul McCartney played bass for the Beatles, but the unknowing fan would simply say that he played guitar. When people spotted Mitch lugging his forty-pound stand-up model through a hotel doorway, they jumped out of the way in a hurry.

"I didn't learn to play the bass until just right before we got ready to go out on the road. When I made the decision to become a member of the Dillards, the only instrument they needed was a bass, so Rodney, Dean and Douglas taught me how to play the bass. Those guys could play almost anything," he asserted.

Mitch was born July 4, 1928, in Hammond, Indiana. Although the first two years of his life were spent in a suburb of Chicago, Mitch steadfastly claims Missouri as his natural home state. "Never let the facts get in the way of a good story," a famous person once said. A weaver of tall tales, Mitch has earned his living by this credo. An insignificant piece of paper like a birth certificate might insist that Mitch was born in Indiana rather than Missouri, but that doesn't make it right. This same birth certificate would have the unsuspecting reader believe that Mitch was born at the stroke of midnight on July 5th, rather than a minute or two earlier on July 4th. If the birth certificate was accurate, then why, Mitch argues, does everyone shoot off fireworks to celebrate his birthday on July 4th?

Mitch's father, Augustus Sears Jayne was a lawyer. He and his wife, Bea Jayne, raised Mitch and his older siblings Marilyn and Sears Jayne.

"Mine was not a musical family, although all of us children took piano lessons. My mother was very much into the classics and got us listening to classical music when we were quite small," Mitch said. "My appreciation for classical music has stayed with me all my life. When I was growing up I knew a lot

more about Stravinsky than I did Bill Monroe, but
then again, Bill Monroe hadn't even developed bluegrass by that time."

Playing the piano never sparked any great emo-
tion in Mitch. Growing up in Kahoka, Missouri, he
felt himself constantly pulled by the outdoors. Activ-
ities such as baseball, fishing, and exploring creek
beds required his full attention.

Immediately upon graduation from high school,
Mitch asked for and received his parents' permission
to enlist in the United States Navy. He wanted to sail
the seas, to feel the ocean's breeze on his face and
the gentle slapping of the waves against the ship.
Mitch saw the ocean, but from an altitude of ten
thousand feet. He had landed an unfortunate assignment as a tailgunner on a torpedo bomber stationed
on an aircraft carrier.

He spent the next three years flying backwards in
a constant state of fear—fear of crashing into the
ocean, fear of torpedo bombers in general, and most
of all fear of trying to land a large airplane on a tiny
aircraft carrier that seemed just about the size of a
postage stamp out there in the middle of the ocean.
No matter how many times that Mitch survived the
routine, and no matter how skillful the pilots, the
fear of trying to catch hold of some boat with a land-
ing hook never got any easier. Night landings were
the most frightening of them all.

Mitch swore to God in heaven that if he were allowed to survive his tour of duty, he would never
step aboard another airplane as long as he lived—a
vow he broke the first year the Dillards toured the
country. One year, the group logged more than 100,-
000 air miles.

Riding in a gun turret accompanied only by an empty pair of machine guns offered Mitch plenty of time to contemplate his future. He started writing seriously for the first time, writing about where he had been, since that was what he saw as he flew backward. On board the aircraft carrier, fellow crew members began to recognize Mitch's talent and started putting it to good use.

"Half the guys in my group didn't know how to write and would have me write letters to their girlfriends back home. They would tell me what they wanted to say and I would try to spice it up a bit. I suppose I was the Cyrano De Bergerac of my air group," Mitch laughed.

Having survived the Navy, Mitch returned home and enrolled at Northeast Missouri Teachers College in Kirksville, courtesy of the GI Bill. He spent two years in Kirksville before moving on to the University of Missouri in Columbia. While there he met his future first wife, Lee Detheridge. Meeting Lee would forever change Mitch's life.

Lee was from the Ozarks, born in a log cabin in Owls Bend on the Current River. She enthralled Mitch with stories of growing up in the mountains, of one-room schoolhouses, and most importantly of the people who populated the Ozarks. The more Mitch listened, the more he discovered himself starved for the Ozarks. He realized that this seeming Garden of Eden was where he belonged. During his final semester at the university, Mitch drove to Salem and applied for a teaching position in a one-room schoolhouse. When the community agreed to hire Mitch, he quit school and moved to the Ozarks.

Mitch spent the next three years performing before captive audiences at Cross School on Horse Creek. He quickly fell in love with his young pupils—with the poetic, antiquated form of Middle English that they spoke, and with their natural curiosity about the world around them. His teaching career would eventually prepare him for life on radio and the stage.

"I've always been comfortable performing in public, which I think came from teaching. When you stand in a schoolroom and teach kids all day long it makes you a performer," Mitch explained. "I learned public speaking by teaching groups of fifteen or twenty kids in one-room schoolhouses such as the Cross School. Teachers in those days became almost like a thespian. A teacher acted out things, described things, drew pictures on the board, and was a lecturer."

When classes weren't in session, the school house was used as a meeting place for women to put up their quilting frames, for farmers to discuss politics, or for church congregations to gather. The school was where the county nurse came to immunize the residents of the community, and where the county agent taught farmers how to grow corn on rocky land. There were dances, weddings, pie suppers, and community get-togethers. Life revolved around this humble building, but then one day it suddenly went away under the guise of progress.

Mitch taught mountain children for four years. School consolidation in 1953 left Mitch with a career decision: he could adopt the new way of teaching, where teachers taught one subject to large classes eight hours a day, or look for another job. He decided to try his hand at radio.

Mitch continues to grieve over the demise of those humble schools.

"I've always maintained that consolidation of the one-room schools was one of the less fortunate things that we have done in all of our wisdom. Consolidation was done for all the right reasons. We wanted to afford more and better teachers, to provide better books and to build better all-around schools in terms of air-conditioned or heated schools. All of that stuff was true and well meaning, but it came with sacrifices as well.

"They built big schools designed to hold a couple hundred to maybe five hundred children. Classes were suddenly larger, and teachers lost the ability to pay attention to each particular child and their individual needs. The one-room schoolhouses, I still think, provided the most effective one-on-one teaching method that has ever been found in this or any other country. Of course they are no longer practical, but during their time they offered the most wonderful teaching methods ever devised by man," Mitch contends.

Mitch went to work for KSMO, a little 250-watt radio station in Salem, Missouri, smack dab in the middle of the Ozark Mountains. The station, located at the intersection of Main and Hickory Street, was a "Mom and Pop" business owned and managed by Bill and Irene Smith. The couple wore nearly every hat in the operation—they were on-the-air announcers, advertising sales representatives, and managers of the station's daily operations. Bill and Irene were desperate for announcers, and in 1953 hired Mitch on a part-time basis while he finished his final year of teaching.

"Working in radio was a lot like lecturing in the classroom, only the audience was larger. I couldn't see their faces, since I was only talking into a piece of metal, but I knew who was listening. I knew all their names and I knew their kids, because I taught most of them. I gave them the best road to take into town when the creeks were up, and told them if the school buses were running. When I started out as a full-time announcer I think I was earning seventy-five dollars a week, which was more than I made as a teacher. By the time I left the radio station I was making the top pay, one hundred dollars a week," Mitch said.

Two of Mitch's loyal listeners were Rodney and Douglas Dillard. They loved listening to Mitch spin his yarns across the air waves, as much as they enjoyed the music. One day the boys visited Mitch at the station, and a friendship was born.

"Rodney and Douglas used to come by the radio station when they learned that I was interested in bluegrass. I probably played more bluegrass music than anyone else in the area, and I encouraged the boys to come by the station whenever they had the chance. They were good fellas, and boy, were they talented. Rodney and Douglas would bring me records to play, or stop by just to talk about some bluegrass picker they had just heard. Eventually they came out and played at my house. Rodney knew that I was interested in learning to play the banjo, so I swapped him a dog and an old .22-caliber pistol for banjo lessons. He taught me the basics, not three-finger picking, mind you, but how to frail the banjo, so I could go and play with an old fiddler friend of mine named Howe Teague. Howe and I would play

Howe Teague
passed on the art
of storytelling to
Mitch Jayne.
*—photo courtesy of
Mitch Jayne*

at pie suppers and country dances and the like. I wanted to join Howe, because I loved going out and seeing what those people were like, and finding out first hand what the music was like. Playing the banjo gave me an excuse to go along," Mitch said.

Rodney argues that Mitch turned out to be the better horse trader of the pair. A more apt description of Mitch's wheeling and dealing might be that of a used car salesman.

"Max was a terrible dog and our relationship was extremely short-lived. He was always trying his best to eat my horse and every cow in the county. Mitch definitely got the better end of the deal," Rodney said with a laugh.

The best education for Mitch came from listening to other musicians. He traveled the state with friends whenever word reached Salem that some bluegrass picker was receiving rave reviews.

"Missouri is not that huge, and every bluegrass

picker knew just about every other bluegrass picker.
If you heard that somebody was pretty good, before
long everybody had heard about him. It wasn't un-
common for us to drive one hundred or two hundred miles to somebody's house just to play with
them and to see first hand if they were really that
good, and hopefully to learn what they knew. Besides, bluegrass is fun music and it is just as much
fun to play with strangers as it is friends you've
known all your life," Mitch said.

This close circle of bluegrass musicians resulted
in the formation of the Dillards.

Rodney, Douglas and Dean wrote and practiced
songs daily on the back porch of Mitch's house.
Meanwhile, a radio station in St. Louis offered Mitch
an announcer's position at the princely sum of five
hundred dollars a week. The time to decide whether
the group was going to make a serious attempt at
success in music was at hand. This meant going on
the road in hopes of finding work, fame, and (perhaps) fortune. Mitch shunned the radio station's offer and cast his lot with his young friends. Bluegrass
music was gaining popularity. Dozens of bands were
popping up throughout the country, and in some
cases it was difficult to distinguish one band from
another. The Dillards realized immediately that if the
band was going to have a shot at success, they would
have to offer something different.

I'll Never See My Home Again

A logjam of struggling bluegrass bands based in Nashville swayed the group to look elsewhere for fame and fortune. Earlier, the group had met Peter Weston, an avid bluegrass fan. Weston's passion revolved around collecting the sounds of bluegrass. So insatiable was Weston's appetite for music that he had built a recording studio in his house. Weston invited the Dillard brothers and Webb to his home to cut a demo record and the group jumped at the chance. Inside the homemade studio the band recorded tunes which would later become Dillard standards—songs such as "Groundhog," "Reubens Train" and "Banjo in the Hollow."

Nearly thirty-five years later, Dean continues to long for the release of that original tape, in order to give fans an opportunity to catch the raw energy of the young band.

The demo record gave the band a chance to audition on the West Coast without the expense of travel. With the group's record tucked safely away in his belongings, Mitch accompanied his family to Los Angeles for a combination vacation and scouting expedition. Mitch's sister, Marilyn, lived in California and worked for KTLA in Los Angeles. Through Marilyn, Mitch had met Norman Malkin, a publisher and personal manager. Malkin agreed to circulate the demo tape to the various clubs around the Los Angeles area in an effort to attract interest in the Dillards.

Brimming with optimism fueled by Malkin's favorable response, Mitch returned to Salem with renewed determination and zeal. Fully expecting to be summoned to California at any second, the boys devoted their undivided attention to rehearsing songs penned by Mitch, Dean and the Dillards, and raising funds for the trip.

Only essential possessions like Rodney's rifle, which they used to hunt their dinner, were kept. Everything else was sold to raise money for the future trip west.

"We shot deer and wild turkey for food to stay alive," Rodney explained. "One day Mitch brought in this tremendous turkey and I've got to say right here, it didn't look all that wild. I've got a feeling that one of Mitch's neighbors is probably still wondering what happened to his turkey."

Mitch fervently denies the charge, but is quick to add that if a turkey, wild or otherwise, happened to answer his call, it got shot.

Time passed at a snail's pace with no word coming from California. They telephoned Malkin repeatedly but always received the same response—be patient. When the band felt they could no longer subdue the urge to head for the Hollywood hills, Rodney sold his car and rifle for sixty dollars. The money paid for a one-wheel trailer to haul the band's meager belongings.

"You have to remember that we were as green as

grass. We had given the demo tape to Malkin and couldn't understand why clubs weren't knocking down our door begging us to come play," Dean said. "We didn't know just how competitive the business was and still is. Finally, we got tired of waiting, called Malkin and said, 'Hey, we're coming to California.' Norman tried desperately to convince us to stay put, but we were determined to leave Missouri."

Mitch, Lee and the couple's children drove to Dallas, Texas, while the rest of the group charted a course for Oklahoma near the end of November, 1963. The plan called for Mitch to remain with his family until the band secured a job. The trailer, hitched to Dean's 1955 Cadillac, was overflowing with clothes, instruments, food and people. The vehicle resembled a primitive South American native bus traveling from village to village, lacking only mattresses, squawking chickens and nervous goats to complete the wild picture.

Charged with enthusiasm and the thrill of adventure, the Dillards and Dean managed to squeeze their bodies into the car. An aunt brought the Dillards a Thanksgiving turkey as a going away present and waved good-bye as the boys chugged off toward Oklahoma. The band would soon realize how difficult a task they had ahead of them.

Car troubles along the way seriously damaged the group's fragile financial status. By the time the band limped into Oklahoma City they were nearly flat broke. Exhausted from the journey, the group parked in the middle of an oil field and settled in for the night. Before going to sleep they cracked open the car windows, paying scant attention to the whistling wind swirling around the car. Awakening

The Dillards in the early days. (l-r) Rodney Dillard, Douglas Dillard
and Mitch Jayne with Dean Webb in front.
—*photo courtesy of the Dillards*

the following morning, the novice travelers learned
an interesting tidbit about Oklahoma. It possesses
vast amounts of red soil which filters through car
windows rather easily. The band bore a striking resemblance to over-painted Indians in a Hollywood B-
western.

Instead of no-vacancy signs, the band discovered
there were plenty of hotel and motel rooms available.
Unfortunately, these all required a sizable amount of
cash. A check of the treasury revealed the group's re-
serves had dwindled down to nine dollars and fifty
cents. One member of the band secured a room at
the local YMCA and the others sneaked in unnoticed

by management. The room contained two single beds, which posed minor logistical problems for a three-member band. This was solved by wiring the two beds together so all three could sleep a bit more comfortably.

Having settled into their temporary quarters, the boys scoured the community in search of a nightclub requiring the services of a bluegrass band. They made the rounds daily, but the polite response was always the same, "Sorry, no openings." Meanwhile, the boys were amassing a hefty bill at the YMCA. Worse yet, food was becoming uncomfortably scarce, the daily fare consisting of crackers and ketchup. Lost in the excitement of the trip was the memory of the Thanksgiving turkey still waiting patiently for them in the trailer.

Desperate for cash, the two brothers wandered into the Red Cross and offered to sell their blood, but found no takers. "Rodney and I tried to sell our blood once, but we were turned down," Douglas said shaking his head as he recounted tales from harder days. "A fella told us that the Red Cross would pay us for blood so we walked down there, but they wouldn't take it because we weren't residents."

Letters from the folks in Salem were less than sympathetic. Aunt Dollie McNeil once wrote Rodney and Douglas begging them to return to Salem. She warned that they were going a long way to flop, and they could fail just as easily in the comfort of their own home. Despite the hardships, no one mentioned the possibility of turning back to Salem.

"The thought never crossed our minds. Hey, to me it was like I was some cowboy riding the range.

It was all part of a grand adventure," Rodney explained.

Down to their last buck-fifty, and with no immediate job prospects in sight, the time had arrived for drastic action. Unknown to the rest of the group, Rodney gambled. He spent the last of their funds on a haircut.

"The idea was to make me look as presentable as possible, and then for me to find everyone jobs. When I got back the guys were really mad at first. They couldn't believe that I had spent the last of the food money. But by going to Manpower Temporary Services, I somehow managed to wrangle us all odd jobs. We carried office equipment, set up voting machines and stacked license plates," Rodney said. "Our first television appearance wasn't on *The Andy Griffith Show*, but on the evening news, during a segment showing workers setting up voting machines."

"We took every odd job imaginable to keep from either starving or freezing to death," Dean added. "We simply couldn't find (music) work anywhere, and it looked like we were never going to get out of Oklahoma City."

Salvation came in the form of a cancellation at the Buddhi Club. The club's owner, Pop Brainard, auditioned the band and was impressed. He then asked the boys something they had never really considered: "How much money do you want?"

Rodney meekly asked for two hundred a week, if it wasn't too much trouble. Brainard shook his head and told them he couldn't offer them anything less than three hundred a week plus a free room.

A telephone call brought Mitch scurrying up from Texas, and the band was together for their first professional road show. Living upstairs over a beer joint had certain disadvantages. When the Dillards went to bed for the night, many of the revelers were still getting wound up. As the band tried to sleep, the patrons kept the party going by cranking up the jukebox.

"The jukebox would nearly blow you out of bed, but the place was warm and you could cook meals there, which was cheaper than eating out every day or eating at the Y," Dean chuckled.

By the end of the week the Buddhi was jumping, and the Dillards were performing before packed audiences. Brainard rewarded the Dillards with a hundred-dollar bonus. Money in hand, the band had a large enough grubstake to finish the trip to California.

Hardship struck again outside of Winslow, Arizona, when Rodney became deathly ill and lost his voice. When they reached Los Angeles one sunny morning, the boys were amazed to find a city surrounded by wildlife and greenery. The calm was broken by rush hour traffic.

"We'd been in some big cities before, but we had never seen anything like rush hour traffic in Los Angeles. It was pretty unnerving," Rodney recalled.

Rodney was still sick when they arrived. Before exploring the city, the band secured Rodney a cheap room at the Melrose Motel in a not so nice section of Melrose Avenue.

"The place was pretty much hooker heaven. The motel was sleazy and the walls paper thin," Rodney said reflecting on those early days. "I was still sick and hearing all of these wild things going on in the rooms around me. I thought that this was where I was going to die."

About this time, the boys also began to notice a foul odor coming from the trailer. The smell in fact came from a fowl—the Thanksgiving turkey given to them as a going-away present. The group buried the bird behind a restaurant.

Given all the trials and tribulations of their journey, the events of the next couple of weeks would resemble a fairy tale—or a dream sequence that no member of the original Dillards would ever forget.

After cleaning up a bit at the Melrose, the boys (minus Rodney) headed into the city in eager pursuit of fame and fortune. They landed at the door of the Ash Grove, a popular hangout for poets, beatniks, folk singers and bluegrass musicians. Appearing that night was a New York-based bluegrass band, the Greenbriar Boys. Prior to leaving Missouri, Dean had chanced upon an article featuring these New Yorkers in the bluegrass magazine *Broadside*. Dean remembered the band from the magazine story, and told his companions that they should introduce themselves to their fellow bluegrass musicians.

Dean, Mitch and Douglas struck an immediate friendship with the Greenbriar Boys; before the evening was through Rodney had rejoined the group and the two bands were jamming on stage. Seated in the audience that night was Jim Dickson, a talent scout and producer for Elektra Records. Dickson, who produced such musical acts as the Byrds, was duly impressed by the novel sound of the Dillards and afterward approached them.

"Jim introduced himself to us and then asked if

we were planning on playing at the Ash Grove on the following night," Dean recalled. "We told him that if they would have us back, then we would play."

Dickson then caught the Dillards off guard with a startling offer. He proposed to convince Jac Holzman, the head of Elektra Records, to accompany him to the club to hear the Dillards. The boys were flabbergasted by this incredible turn of events. The next night, Holzman listened to the show and concurred with Dickson that there was something uniquely special about the Dillards. Holzman and the Dillards met after the show and the band inked their first recording contract.

Elektra's discovery merited merely a tiny blurb in *Daily Variety*, noting simply that the record company had signed a fledgling bluegrass band from Missouri. The snippet created few ripples of excitement within the entertainment community, but timing is indeed everything. Unknown to the Dillards, Jim Fritzell and Everett Greenbaum, the script-writing comic geniuses behind *The Andy Griffith Show*, were hammering out a script that would alter the band's destiny. They had penned a story line which required the services of an imaginary, musically-inclined mountain family—the Darlings.

The Darlin Boys

"The Dillards and the Darlings were two horses that were kept in the same stable. The Darlings became the flip side of the Dillards."
—Mitch Jayne

Jim Fritzell and Everett Greenbaum had yet to flesh out the Darling characters, but they knew the show would require the services of a cantankerous father, his big, lanky sons, and a flirtatious daughter. The *Daily Variety* piece on the Dillards attracted the curious attention of Richard Linke, associate producer of *The Andy Griffith Show*, who wondered if these Missourians could transform themselves into the Darling family. Linke contacted Elektra Records management and arranged to audition the band.

Before the group could comprehend the chain of events unfolding, they were whisked away to Desilu Studios. Huddled on the set of *The Andy Griffith Show*, Griffith, director Bob Sweeney and series producer Aaron Ruben eyeballed the young musicians and chatted quietly amongst themselves. Once the conference ended, according to Dean, Griffith nodded in the direction of the Dillards and remarked, "Do something for us, boys."

"We played about half a tune and Andy stopped it right there. He talked with some crew members for a while, then he walked over to us. He said we

Buckskin Darlings—The flip side of the Darlings, the Dillards pose in a rare promotional photograph with Andy Griffith inside Sheriff Taylor's home.   —*photo courtesy of Douglas Dillard*

looked right and sounded right and they offered us a job. Thirty years have passed, and every time I think about that first few weeks in Hollywood it still amazes me. Here we nearly starved to death in Oklahoma City, and within such a short period of time after hitting Hollywood, we had ourselves our first gig, a record deal, and then a television spot. It sounded more like a movie script than real life," Dean said, recalling that magical moment in time.

Years later Mitch pondered Griffith's selection of the Dillards and came to the conclusion that Griffith was searching for more than four guys who happened to play bluegrass music. Griffith, Mitch contends, was also looking for interesting faces, body language and overall physical appearance.

"The fact that we were all kind of long and rangy and rural-looking and all had interesting faces played into his decision," Mitch reasoned. "Musically we were probably playing at our peak, because we were auditioning nearly every night and auditioning keeps you sharp. Andy wanted the music, but he was also looking for people who fit the physical image."

The boys' enthusiasm was tempered by reluctance to appear on television as ignorant hillbillies. Rodney in particular had always insisted that the band avoid the Hollywood stereotypical view of mountain folk.

"Performers like Judy Canova had depicted rural Americans as people who wore clothes with straw sticking out from everywhere and those ridiculous pointed hats," Dean explained. "Rural people, to the Hollywood crowd, were considered hayseeds, and Rodney resented that image. Our view was that country people, no matter how backwoodsy they were, carried a certain dignity about them and in their work. Rodney wanted to make sure that we weren't going to be making fun of the people we grew up with."

Thirty-five years after the fact, Rodney Dillard continues to question the band's decision.

"You know, I still have reservations about accepting the role as the Darlings," Rodney said. "Of course, in retrospect our performances as the Darling family have lasted longer than anything else we've done since, but I still wonder if it was the right thing to do."

Rodney's initial misgivings were soon erased. The Dillards started rehearsals and sowed the seeds of what would grow into lifelong friendships with their

co-stars, Denver Pyle and Maggie Peterson, a talented singer discovered by Linke when the Colorado
native was only a teenager.

Hearing Denver Pyle declare, "Everybody on the
truck!" sounded vaguely familiar to Maggie Peterson. The young actress/singer who wowed audiences
with her looks, energy and beautiful voice as Charlene Darling, knew all about dilapidated pick-up
trucks.

Maggie Peterson began her career at age ten,
along with her brother Jim Peterson, as one-half of
the Ja Da Quartet. The Dixieland jazz band broke
into the business with Maggie as the lead singer,
playing for any local civic club or event willing to
listen.

"We had a 1922 red Model-A Ford pickup truck
that we drove everywhere," she said with a laugh.
"They'd throw the banjo, drums and me into the
back of the truck and off we would go."

Her association with Andy Griffith began indi-
rectly at age thirteen, when the quartet left their
homes in Greeley, Colorado in search of fame and
fortune. The group headed to the resort community
of Estes Park, Colorado, intent on taking the town by
storm. Brimming with excitement and confidence,
they landed a job at the Stanley Hotel.

"We were young, cute, preppie, and maybe pretty good," Maggie said shyly. "We packed the audiences in that summer. Well, Capitol Records held
their convention there, and several of the people
from their New York offices came by and caught our
show. Dick Linke was among the Capitol people who
saw us perform."

Intrigued and impressed by the youngsters' talent, Linke urged the group to visit him if they ever managed to reach New York. Linke's invitation echoed in Maggie's ears for the next few years. When high school graduation finally arrived, Maggie and the group made a beeline to New York and landed on Linke's doorstep.

"Dick remembered us and got us an audition on *The Perry Como Show*. We auditioned and a couple of days later we were asked to come on the show along with Gary Cooper and Lena Horne," Maggie said. "They received a lot of good mail about our performance, and we were asked to come back twice."

Pat Boone caught the quartet's act and invited the group to appear as regulars on his show for a season. When the group wasn't performing in New York they were traveling extensively throughout the country. Eventually the boys tired of performing, and Jim Peterson decided to return to college. He later followed his father's footsteps and became a physician.

By this time, Linke and Andy Griffith were developing *The Andy Griffith Show*. Maggie had met Griffith through Linke in 1961, but never realized she would one day be working with him.

When the part of Charlene Darling was written, Linke remembered Maggie and summoned her to California to read for it. Maggie was singing in Scottsdale, Arizona at the time, but flew to California to audition. The pairing of the Dillards and Maggie Peterson was a perfect fit from the start, as the fictional family formed an immediate kinship.

"We shared the same sense of humor and appreciation for music. I love bluegrass music, because of the honesty in the music. There was nothing phony about the Dillards or their music," she asserted. "I've always felt like they were my brothers. We might go for years without seeing one another, but when we are together it is like we have never been apart. They are all excellent musicians and wrote some beautiful and clever songs. Rodney has a beautiful voice and is the one who brings it all together. He and Frank Sinatra are my favorite singers. Mitch is a wonderful storyteller. Douglas' expertise on the banjo is just marvelous. He would sit around the set and just knock everybody out with his playing. Dean is the adorable one. The mandolin was made for him."

The Dillards shared a similar affection for Maggie Peterson.

"She was the most delightful friend to have on that set. She identified with all of us guys, because she had grown up with this big brother who was into music too. Around the third Darling episode we filmed, Maggie very shyly showed us the butterfly that she had tattooed on her toe. Her showing us her tattoo was a real family-type thing," Mitch recalled.

Maggie breaks into laughter when the butterfly becomes the topic of discussion.

"It takes a while for me to get to know someone well enough to show them my tattoo," she chuckled. "When I sang, I used to dance with my shoes off. Everybody thought I had a dirty big toe, but actually they were seeing my butterfly tattoo."

Maggie obtained the dainty butterfly on a spur of the moment impulse while performing in Juarez, Mexico. Wandering around the marketplace, she came across a tattoo parlor. She peered into the window and noticed dozens of beautiful examples of tat-

too art. Moments later, she painfully found herself
the proud owner of a tiny butterfly.

"It hurt," Maggie declared. "I couldn't put on my
shoes for a couple of nights. What really surprised
me was my parents' reaction. When my mother saw
it, I expected her to be upset, but instead she said,
'Isn't that cute.' My dad, on the other hand, looked
at it and said, 'I can remove that if you want.' But it
is still with me today."

Few snails and turtles, Mitch asserts, manage to
move at a pace slower than the filming of a television series. The boys kept themselves and the others
on the set entertained with improvised concerts. Lee
Greenway, the show's makeup man and a banjo picker himself, would occasionally play along with the
Dillards. Once the music got going, Griffith, who
kept his own instruments tucked away inside his
dressing room, would find a place to jump in and
hang on tight.

"Andy was very businesslike on the set, but he
always found the time to play a few songs with us,"
Mitch noted.

Dean has a particular fondness for Greenway, as
his character, Other Darling (pronounced Othor),
was named for Greenway as an inside joke.

"In that first episode, *The Darlings Are Coming*,
there is a scene where the Darlings have snuck into
the hotel room. Briscoe is about to pull up the rope
when Charlene says, 'What about Other?' I was the
only person not in the hotel room scene, so naturally
that meant that I must be Other. Other was Lee
Greenway's middle name. They threw it out there in-
tentionally as part of the dialogue just so they could
catch Lee's reaction."

Time to breathe, time for music: A rare glimpse inside the Darling homestead in a scene from *Mountain Wedding.* —*photo courtesy of Mitch Jayne*

Wedding night jitters: The Darling family show concern over Sheriff Taylor's ailing foot in a scene from *Divorce Mountain Style.* —*photo courtesy of Douglas Dillard*

The Look: The Darling boys reunite in Nashville. *—photo courtesy of Douglas Dillard*

Maggie, Rodney and Don Knotts
in Nashville.
*—photo courtesy of
Douglas Dillard*

Other and Jebbin Darling
(Dean & Doug)
get into character during
Return to Mayberry.
*—photo courtesy of
Douglas Dillard*

Old friends: The Dillards, Maggie Peterson and Mr. & Mrs. Andy Griffith on the set of *Return to Mayberry*. —*photo courtesy of Douglas Dillard*

The Darlings try to get a marriage license from county clerk Howard Sprague (the late Jack Dodson), on the set of *Return to Mayberry*.
—*photo courtesy of Douglas Dillard*

ACTORS TELEVISION MOTION PICTURE
MINIMUM THREE-DAY CONTRACT

Continuous Employment—Three-day Basis—Three-day Salary—Three-day Minimum Employment

THIS AGREEMENT made this ___4th___ day of ___FEBRUARY___, 19 __63__, between
__MAYBERRY ENTERPRISES_____, a corporation, hereinafter called "Producer,"
and _____DEAN WEBB_____, hereinafter called "Player,"

WITNESSETH:

1. *Photoplay, Role and Guarantee.* Producer hereby engages Player to render service as such in the role of
__"WARD DARLING"_____, in a photoplay produced primarily for exhibition
over free television, the working title of which is now __"THE DARLINGS ARE COMING"___ #25-C (88)
Player accepts such engagement upon the terms herein specified. Producer guarantees that it will furnish Player not less than
_____3_____ day's employment. (If this blank is not filled, the guarantee shall be three days.)

2. *Salary and Advances.* The Producer will pay to the Player, and the Player agrees to accept for three (3) days (and pro rata for each additional day beyond three (3) days) compensation as follows:

Three-day salary	($ 255.00)
*Advance for television re-runs	($)
*Advance for theatrical use	($)
Three-day Total (including advances)	($ 255.00)

3. Producer shall have the unlimited right throughout the world to rerun the motion picture on television and exhibit it theatrically.

4. If the motion picture is rerun on television in the United States or Canada and contains any of the results and proceeds of the Player's services, the Player will be paid the amounts entered in the blanks in this paragraph plus an amount equal to one-third (⅓rd) thereof for each day of employment in excess of three (3) days and if the blanks are not filled the Player will be paid the minimum additional compensation prescribed therefor by the 1960 Screen Actors Guild Television Agreement below mentioned, and the amount, if any, designated in Paragraph 2 as an advance for reruns shall be applied against the additional compensation for reruns payable under this Paragraph 4.

2nd run	3rd run	4th run	5th run	6th and all succeeding runs

5. If the motion picture is exhibited theatrically anywhere in the world and contains any of the results and proceeds of the Player's services, the Player will be paid $_____ plus an amount equal to one-third thereof for each day of employment in excess of three (3) days (but in any event the total shall not be less than the minimum required by the 1960 Screen Actors Guild Television Agreement). If this blank is not filled in, the Player will be paid the applicable minimum additional compensation to which he would be entitled under such Television Agreement, and the amount, if any, designated in Paragraph 2 as an advance for theatrical use shall be applied against the additional compensation for theatrical use payable under this Paragraph 5.

6. *Term.* The term of employment hereunder shall begin on __FEBRUARY 4, 1963__
_____, on or about**_____
and shall continue thereafter until the completion of the photography and recordation of said role.

7. *Basic Contract.* Reference is made to the 1960 Screen Actors Guild Television Agreement and to the applicable provisions set forth in such Agreement. Player's employment shall include performance in non-commercial openings,

Ward Darling's (aka Dean Webb) original contract for *The Darlings Are Coming* with Mayberry Enterprizes. Ward never forgot a line of dialogue.
—photo courtesy of Dean Webb

**"Maggie Peterson gets prettier every year,"
Rodney Dillard.**
*—photo courtesy of
Douglas Dillard*

Dean was one of only two Darling boys blessed with a first name in the group's debut. Douglas Dillard was the other fully-named Darling, his first name being Jebbin. The scripts given to the Dillards actually listed the characters' full names but, other than Jebbin none were used. The name on Dean's script wasn't Other, but in fact was Ward Darling. Ironically, in the Dillards' second appearance, *Mountain Wedding*, the final script lists Mitch Jayne as Other Darling. The cast credits listed on the script continue to refer to Dean Webb as Ward Darling (also son number three) and Douglas Dillard as Jebbin Darling (son number two). Rodney Dillard's character's name is Frankie Darling. Later, in Episode 193, *The Darling Fortune*, Griffith casually refers to the Dillards by their real first names.

Musicians possessing a keen eye for detail might spot an editing slip in *The Darlings Are Coming*. Incorporating songs into each episode was a two-part process, Dean explained. Once musical director Earle Hagan decided on the tunes to be played, the Dillards pre-recorded the songs. Later, when the music scenes were filmed, a transcription record was played and the Dillards pretended to play their instruments. During the editing process, the pre-recorded songs and the film were synchronized. A flub occurred in a close-up shot of Douglas' fiery banjo picking fingers. Douglas' fingers are playing "Banjo in the Hollow," but the music heard is "Salty Dog Blues."

Denver Pyle never actually played the jug in *The Darlings Are Coming*. Instead, a musician was employed to play water bottles, which were then mixed in with the Dillards' own picking. The Dillards later requested that the jug sound be kept out of future episodes. The request was granted, and the water bottle accompaniment did not return until the made for television movie *Return to Mayberry*. While scenes in subsequent original episodes depict Pyle playing the jug, no sound is actually heard. The visual image of Pyle's enthusiastic juggin' leaves the viewer with the illusion that the sound is actually present in the song, Douglas explained.

Another trivia item for Dillards fans involves the title "Doug's Tune." Douglas had written the song shortly after the group reached California, but had never gotten around to naming the piece. During one scene, Briscoe Darling asks Sheriff Taylor what song he would like to play. Andy Griffith responds with, "How about Doug's Tune?" The name stuck.

The Darlings Are Coming ranks as Maggie's favorite appearance, as it represented something completely original.

"Everyone was so full of energy. It was an eye-opener and a landmark event for myself and the Dillards," she said. "I remember when we filmed that first scene coming into town on the truck. When the truck stopped they stopped the camera, and I thought that was it. I didn't realize you had to do wide-angle shots, long shots and close ups."

Filming complete, the boys' first television appearance as the Darlings was in the can. Word of the group's sudden fame quickly reached friends and relatives in Salem. When *The Darlings Are Coming* aired on March 8, 1963, the Salem National Guard unit went home early so everyone could watch the hometown boys.

"We didn't realize that a network television show would give you so much notoriety. Of course, we were still fresh off the truck," Douglas Dillard remembered.

The Dillards and the Darlings have been inseparable ever since.

When the Dillards accepted *The Andy Griffith Show* job they reckoned it would be a one-time appearance, so they tried to get their best licks in. Once the episode aired, however, the boys were impressed by the show and hoped to be invited for a return engagement.

"We were pretty proud of ourselves after that first show, and we felt that we would be asked to come back," Mitch recalled.

They were. Audience response to the Darling family was extremely favorable and the mountain family was quickly summoned back to Mayberry a month later for Episode 94, entitled *Mountain Wedding*. The Darlings invaded Mayberry a total of six times during the series' run. Episode 100, *Briscoe Declares for Aunt Bee*, featured Denver Pyle serenading to his sweetheart, Aunt Bee. Dean accepted the assignment of finding just the right song for Pyle to croon.

"Denver reminded me a lot of Roy Acuff. My brother had this old Roy Acuff songbook once, so I went to a music shop and dug around until I found a copy. I flipped through the book for a while and hit on "Low and Lonely." I thought it would be the perfect song for a man like Briscoe Darling to sing, and it really worked out well," Dean said.

The episode marked the first time that Pyle, already a veteran film and television actor, had ever been asked to sing on camera.

"I was scared to death," Pyle recalled with a

laugh. "I've got an ear for music, but I'm not a singer. I would start in one key then move on to somewhere else, but they somehow managed to piece it all together."

Briscoe Declares for Aunt Bee is especially dear to Pyle, because it afforded him the opportunity to work closely with Frances Bavier.

"Frances was a true actress. She never slipped out of character. Her performance was always very solid and she gave you something to work against. When I directed the last three years of *The Doris Day Show*, we would have experienced actors and actresses come on the set worried about being in a comedy and getting laughs. They would say, 'I've never played in a comedy.' We would always tell them, 'Don't worry about the laughs, just play the character and Doris will make you funny.' That was how it was with Frances. She possessed a natural ability to react to you, and to be in tune with you, that she would help you say what you wanted to say as an actor."

Whenever possible, Griffith allowed the Dillards to perform their own material on the shows. By playing original compositions such as "Ebo Walker" and "Doug's Tune," the boys profited from mechanical royalties each time one of their songs was played on television. The original script for *Briscoe Declares for Aunt Bee* included the Dillards performing an off-camera radio commercial for Big Hog Corn Mash. The stage direction for the scene notes that the "Darlings" (not the Dillards) can "record this when they're recording the other tunes." The following is the proposed commercial, which was cut from the final version:

Sooooooweeeeee, pig pig!
Sooooooweeeeee, pig pig!
Pig, pig, dance a jig,
Happy, healthy, happy little pig.
Big Hog Corn Mash in your bin,
Fills you up with vigor and vim . . .
Pig, pig, dance a jig,
Happy, healthy, happy little pig.
(spells)
B-I-G H-O-G. That spells Big Hog.
The mash of healthy pigs. Get
some today! Tell 'em Hog Wallace
sent you . . . you hear???

Singing offered audiences the infrequent opportunity to match a voice with the character's face. Performing original and traditional bluegrass songs had a side benefit as well. Like Lester Flatt and Earl Scruggs, who occasionally performed as themselves on *The Beverly Hillbillies*, the Dillards' appearances on *The Andy Griffith Show* introduced bluegrass music to unsuspecting audiences who otherwise never would have considered listening to it.

The only instance in which the boys are heard to talk ironically came in the band's first appearance. During one scene in *The Darlings Are Coming*, the boys are locked up inside the Mayberry Jail and have just finished a dinner provided by Aunt Bee. As Aunt Bee leaves the courthouse, the boys in unison bid her goodnight and thank her for supper. Since the boys are all speaking at once, it is nearly impossible to match the voices to the players. Mitch Jayne can be heard to say that he's "about to pop," while Douglas Dillard is credited with the line, "Great Beans, Aunt Bee," the latter of which has since become a *TAGS* fan club chapter name. Although the

The Darlings Are Coming—The Darlings descend on Mayberry.
Back row, the Dillards; front, Maggie Peterson and Denver
Pyle.   —*photo courtesy of Douglas Dillard*

boys rarely spoke, the language of the Ozarks managed to sneak into the filming. Denver Pyle would
occasionally use sayings borrowed from the Dillards
such as, "We'll scrub one off for ya," which trans-
lated means that the boys will gladly play another
tune.

Nearly all the scripts called for the boys to speak
via facial expressions. The impassive stares of the
Darling boys coupled with Briscoe's lines (such as

"Can't ya see just how excited they all are?") added to the humor and the band's character. Douglas, often described on stage by Mitch as constantly grinning like a possum eating bumblebees, is the only Dillard ever caught smiling on camera. During the jail scene in *The Darlings Are Coming* the impassive face of Jebbin Darling breaks into a momentary grin before quickly slipping back into his normal stoic stare.

While all of the episodes were filled with laughter, Mitch and Pyle agree that their favorite episode was *Mountain Wedding*. The show includes a scene involving the Darling family asleep in their cabin while Andy and Barney are awake and on guard duty trying to keep a watchful eye out for Ernest T. Bass, played by Howard Morris. The script called for the Darlings to snore loudly, and the Dillards did their best to cooperate.

"Denver would give three big snorts and then lay there dead," Mitch laughed as he recounted the scene. "Douglas would grunt like a pig. Rodney would snort and snuffle. Dean sounded like a lung patient in traction, and I got going doing horse lip noises. We cracked Andy and Don up, just tore them to pieces. Andy fell out of his chair laughing. It took all morning to get it out of their system and film that little scene. The laughter was so infectious that when we finally did get the shot, I still had to put my hand over my face to keep from laughing."

Mountain Wedding is special to Maggie, as it marked the first time that she worked with Don Knotts. They even shared the same wedding dress.

"Don and I wore the same wedding dress and it

fit us both perfectly. They didn't have to alter it all for us, which I suppose doesn't say a whole lot for either of our figures," Maggie said with a laugh.

While Charlene Darling's eyes always roamed in the direction of Sheriff Taylor, ironically it was Don Knotts who ultimately captured the girl. When Knotts left the series to pursue his own film career, Maggie Peterson was tabbed to play his girlfriend and future bride in *The Love God*. Peterson later worked with Andy Griffith in the film, *Angel In My Pocket*.

Rehearsals amazed the Dillards. Regulars like Don Knotts and Andy Griffith would play games with their lines, twirling the words around as a form of mental relaxation. Knotts and Griffith would reverse roles—Knotts' character would become the hero, and Andy's character would assume the position of the comic foil who required salvation. Denver Pyle once told Mitch how he learned this trick employed by Griffith and Knotts while working on a western early in his career.

Pyle played only a small role in that film, but his character spoke one key line. He was to alert the good guys that fur smugglers were headed their way. Pyle's shout would immediately follow the massive release of canoes filled with actors preparing to attack the hero's company, which would progress into the biggest fight scene of the film.

When time arrived for Pyle to utter his vital line, his tongue got tangled and twisted around and he screamed, "Here come the smur fugglers!" The next line uttered on the set was "Cut," as the flub meant scrubbing the take and redoing the whole scene. This required hauling the canoes back upriver, reloading all the guns, and placing everyone back into position, Mitch said.

Dart matches helped pass the time on the Griffith show set. Mitch constantly marveled at the contests staged by Knotts and Griffith, especially since Knotts ruled the roost in that arena.

"Making a TV program is probably one of the most boring things I've ever done in my life. So much time is spent setting up lights, moving cables, and setting up the track where the camera is going to run. Out of every hour spent on a TV set, maybe five minutes is actually dedicated to shooting the scene. Don and Andy killed a lot of time throwing darts in between setups. Don was a dynamite dart thrower. Andy was just a big gandy and would just fling 'em any which way. He didn't have patience, yet he had challenged Don. Don would stand there and concentrate and put it next to the center. Andy would shout, 'Don you hateful puke!' and it would tickle me to death. Here is Don, who is always depicted as being clumsy, while Andy is the guy who is always the super-confident one. When it came to darts, Don Knotts was the guy who was confident and Andy was the guy who just flung 'em," Mitch chortled.

The Dillards had hoped that Andy Griffith would use the boys as his backup band during his various tours. Despite the prosperity of his weekly television series, Griffith continued to tour the nightclub circuit, appearing in resorts such as Las Vegas and Lake Tahoe. The Dillards, much to their dismay, never received the telephone call. Griffith did, however, invite the band to work on a television special which featured himself, Tennessee Ernie Ford and Danny Thomas. The show aired minus Rodney Dillard, who became ill shortly before filming and had to be replaced by Chip Douglas of the Turtles.

The Dillards did reunite with their *TAGS* friends before *Return to Mayberry*. Bob Sweeney, the longtime director of *TAGS*, and Don Knotts later invited the band to appear on Knotts' variety show in the early 1970s.

Encouragement and support also came from Pyle. A fan of bluegrass music and a believer in the Dillards' talent, Pyle used his influence to promote the band at every opportunity. During his stint on *Gunsmoke*, Pyle would periodically invite the Dillards to visit him on the set. He introduced the band to various cast and production members, and the Dillards demonstrated their talent by performing at two cast Christmas parties. Milburn Stone (Doc) and Ken Curtis (Festus) often talked about taking the Dillards on the road with them, but the show never materialized.

The Dillards used references to the Griffith show in their normal club act to illustrate the band's background. Mitch confessed to audiences that no one in the band's hometown expected the boys to succeed. He repeated Aunt Dollie's departing admonition, "You boys are going a long way to flop!" Attitudes in Salem shifted, he added, following the Dillards' debut on *The Andy Griffith Show*.

"Folks back home never believed in the Dillards, but they sure believed in Andy Griffith. They all have plastic statues of Andy Griffith on their dashboards," Mitch explained.

Going Home

Return to Mayberry demonstrated Griffith's continued affection for the series which had secured him a prominent place in the annals of television history. The made-for-television movie offered him the opportunity to reunite old friends, from the regular players such as Ron Howard and Don Knotts to the bit players such as Maggie Peterson, Denver Pyle, and the Dillards. Griffith's genuine appreciation for his co-stars is a common refrain echoed by former cast members during interviews. Mitch's recollections of the actor are no different.

"When we did *Return to Mayberry*, trying to recreate the characters posed some interesting problems for the folks in wardrobe. The men were balding and had pot bellies. They had to try fifty costumes on us in order to make us look like the Darlings again. Somewhere in the process of all those costume changes, I lost my wedding ring," Mitch recalled. "One of the people on the set mentioned this to Andy. Now, Andy always looked after the other people on the show. He came up to me and you could tell he was very concerned. He asked, 'Where do you think you lost it?'

"I explained to him about all the costume changes and told him not to worry, that I would find it eventually. Andy said that he would feel uneasy until we found the ring. He told me, 'What would your wife think about me if I sent you home without your wedding ring?' So the next thing I knew here was this mega-millionaire superstar and me crawling around on our hands and knees, going through trash cans

Back on the truck—The Darling family plus Ernest T. Bass (Howard Morris) in a scene from *Return to Mayberry.*
—*photo courtesy of Douglas Dillard*

and candy wrappers in search of my wedding ring. Andy didn't stop searching until we finally found it."

Return To Mayberry was an amazing undertaking. Twenty years had passed since the Dillards made their final appearance on the show, and the cast members were spread out like a picnic lunch. Dean and Rodney were working in Branson, Douglas had his own band based out of Nashville, and Mitch was in Salem writing books and lecturing on the Ozark language. Ron Howard had gone on to star in *Happy Days* and was becoming one of the most sought-after directors in Hollywood. Howard Morris was directing a film, and Jim Nabors was living in Hawaii. The remaining cast members were living everywhere from New York to Los Angeles. But when asked to return to where it all began, few could refuse.

When the original episodes were filmed, none of the actors could foresee the durability of the show. Yet it was the devotion to detail, character and story development which created classic television. Working on the Griffith show, Maggie Peterson was constantly amazed by the care which went into each piece of dialogue and every scene.

"No one realized it was going to be such a classic television show, but that is how it was treated from the outset. Andy and the writers went to great pains to ensure that every scene was just right. They were so careful that anything that didn't read really funny during the story conferences was taken out and reworked, if necessary. Andy is a very complex man, but he has a great sense of humor," she asserted.

Mayberry and *The Andy Griffith Show* was a favorite spot for Griffith in his career. The actor and his cast all longed to recreate the mystique of Mayberry one last time.

Originally, exterior scenes for *The Andy Griffith Show* were filmed on the back lot of MGM Studios, while interior scenes were shot at Desilu Studios on Cahuenga Boulevard. When *Mayberry RFD* was canceled, both the exterior and interior sets were dismantled and transported on to other jobs like a circus traveling from town to town. The town of Mayberry had been used in everything from feature films to daytime soap operas. Nothing of the original Mayberry existed, except the plans to the town and, perhaps, the magic.

Griffith obtained the plans to the fictitious town and began the hunt for a suitable replacement. Los Olivos, a quiet town in the central part of California, was tabbed as the next Mayberry. Los Olivos was laid out in a beautiful hilly setting which resembled a country scene in rural North Carolina. When community leaders were approached about the possibility of transforming Los Olivos into America's favorite small town, the citizens jumped at the chance.

"They told them, 'We'll pay you and we'll use some of you guys for extras, and your kids in the dance scenes.' Those folks were tickled to death," Mitch said. "They thought it was the most fabulous thing that had ever happened to their town, and maybe it was, too. They took this little town and built fronts across all the existing buildings. They recreated the courthouse and Floyd's Barbershop and the church. They just covered up this entire little town with phony set pieces, then they brought in all of the actors.

Once everything was in place, the call went out for the cast members. Nearly every alumnus arrived in Los Olivos about the same time on the same day, like a great caravan to a family reunion.

"Folks came in vans, tandems, limousines, and we all got out of our vehicles and were dumped onto the Main Street of Mayberry," Mitch said. "We stood there gawking in amazement. There the town was, with a new coat of paint shining in the sun, and the flag run up on the pole in front of the courthouse. It was a heartwarming moment one of the most moving experiences that had happened to me in a long, long time. When I saw how much that little town, which was imaginary in the first place, had gone into the heart of America, that it struck every one of us. Here is where it all started, and it's real. Mayberry is alive again!"

Mitch compared *Return to Mayberry* to a high school class reunion. Unless the former classmates wore name tags the size of a dinner plate, it was sometimes difficult to match a name to a face.

"We went around like that peering at each other. Hal Smith was one of the few people who hadn't changed. He always looked like Otis Campbell. Howie Morris amazed me. He got out of whatever it was he arrived in looking very Hollywood, and within two days they had his teeth all yellow, a two-day growth of beard, his hair all mussed up, and dressed in that ridiculous costume looking like Ernest T. Bass. He got right back into that character, talking and making little asides as if he had always been Ernest T.," Mitch said. "Seeing Betty Lynn and Aneta Corsaut was such a delight. They were always such charming women, and they had retained their beauty."

Maggie Peterson was only twenty-one when she made her debut as Charlene Darling. The years had only changed her for the better, Mitch declared, as she was still just as pretty and bouncy as she was the first time the pair met.

Consistency in the characters' personal history never was a strong suit on the Griffith show. When the series ended Maggie Peterson's character had married Dud Wash, survived rocky moments, and given birth to a daughter, Andelina, named after

Sheriff Taylor. Yet, when *Return to Mayberry* aired, it appeared that Charlene's immediate family had been whisked away into some witness relocation program. Dud Wash and Andelina had both disappeared. Charlene was back at the cabin taking care of her four brothers and Briscoe, and Ernest T. Bass was back trying to court her. So what happened? Even Charlene finds this a true puzzler.

"I wondered about that myself," Maggie remarked. "It looked as though I had spent the last twenty-five years taking care of the boys. I suppose I got myself one of those mountain divorces. But we still had a whee of a time and shared a lot of laughs. It was like we had never been away."

The Dillards received another shock when they noticed a broken-down truck parked across the street. The truck was the original Model-A truck that the Darling family had ridden into town on in the episode *The Darlings Are Coming*, Mitch recalled. Denver Pyle and the Dillards wandered over to the truck and gave it the once-over.

"*Return to Mayberry* was an incredible experience for Andy. I imagine that somewhere in the back of his mind he even wondered, 'Do you suppose we could do this again?' But when he looked at us, he knew that it couldn't be done. This time we were going to do a memory piece and it was going to stick with us all and we would have gotten it out of our system. We were going to recreate that imagery that was Mayberry. In all honesty, *Return to Mayberry* wasn't terribly good, but I still enjoy watching it because I realize how hard we were all trying to make it special. *Return to Mayberry* was really a return for all of us. The magic that Don Knotts and Andy

Griffith possessed had not changed at all. They still just turned each other on and got all those funny little asides and takes that they got off each other," Mitch said.

Viewers apparently shared Mitch's sentiments, as the film received the season's highest rating for a made-for-TV movie and at the time became the seventh highest-rated made-for-TV movie of all time.

The chances of a Darling family reunion tour grow slimmer with each passing year, although there is talk of reuniting the group for a thirty-fifth anniversary celebration of *The Andy Griffith Show*. Fans of the mountain family may, however, one day walk into a record store and make a startling discovery—a collection of songs that made Charlene and Briscoe cry.

Writers Everett Greenbaum and Jim Fritzell took great joy in inventing outlandish song titles such as "Keep Your Money In Your Shoes And It Won't Get Wet" and "Towsack Full Of Love." Greenbaum and Fritzell never managed to get around to actually writing music or lyrics to accompany these gems, and the songs were left to the audience's imagination. Enter Mitch Jayne and Rodney Dillard. Long after The Dillards stopped touring, Mitch and Rodney hit upon the idea of composing original songs for those titles. Lyrics drafted by Mitch now exist for "Never Hit Your Grandma With A Great Big Stick;" "Will You Love Me When I'm Old And Ugly;" and "Tearin' Up Your Old Clothes For Rags," as well as the two titles previously mentioned. Rodney remains in the process of composing the musical score for these destined-to-be-classic Darling numbers. The following are the lyrics and represent the first public presentation of the words that made Charlene cry:

Songs that made Charlene and Briscoe Darling Cry

KEEP YOUR MONEY IN YOUR SHOES
AND IT WON'T GET WET
Lyrics by Mitch Jayne

Up in the mountains peckin' at a hillside
Cookin' that corn mash, skiddin those logs
Pitch a little lovin' and you pitch a little hay
And you throw a little fodder to the durned old hogs.
Mama had a sayin' for the good times—bad times
"Never bitten twice by the same dog yet"
Never saw a dollar, but I heard her say
"Keep your money in your shoes and it won't get wet."

Up in the mountains in the good old days.
Mamma had a sayin' that suited our ways
Told it to me often so I can't forget
"Keep your money in your shoes and it won't get wet."

Mamma knew a lot about the things she said.
"It's pretty sorry skillet that can't find a lid."
"And a high stepper's money won't last till it's gone."
"And you can't get to heaven with the world strapped on."
"And you're huntin' up the devil when you fall in debt."
Keep your money in your shoes, and it won't get wet.

Up in the mountains in the good old days.
Mamma had a sayin' that suited our ways.
Told it to me often, so I can't forget
"Keep your money in your shoes and it won't get wet."

WILL YOU LOVE ME WHEN
I'M OLD AND UGLY
Lyrics by Mitch Jayne

I know that you love me, cause you say that you do.
And lying's not your style,
But till death do us part is a long long time and
The last part takes a while.

In the sweet by and by
When it last it appears
Hair is growing from my ears
Will you love me just the way you did before
In the sweet by and by
Will you leave me a light

When I'm up five times a night
Will you promise not to leave me when I snore.
When I'm old and ugly and my memory's bad
And my temper's getting thin
You can get the picture when you look at my dad
And pretend I look like him.

In the sweet by and by . . .
Will you shout every word,
That you know I haven't heard
Will you wipe away the gravy on my chin
In the sweet by and by
When I can't see too far
And my teeth are in a jar
Will you blame me for the way things might have been.

TEARIN' UP YOUR
OLD CLOTHES
FOR RAGS
Lyrics by Mitch Jayne

You're tearing up your old clothes for rags
The same old clothes were good enough the way you used
    to be
You changed your mind a city mile
And now you're steppin' out in style
But no one fits your size the same as me.

You traded in your old model heart
I found it where you parked it, and it's easy, dear, to start
Just swappin' models doesn't change the road you want to
    re-arrange
The motor's still too good to fall apart

Chorus:
You're tearing up your old clothes for rags
You'll give 'em up for something new
But no one needs them like you do
You're tearing up your old clothes for rags.

TOWSACK FULL OF LOVE
Lyrics by Mitch Jayne

I wrote you a letter on the day you left
And one every day you've been away
And I told you everything I wish I'd said
And the things I wish you'd say
Now you put 'em all unopened in an old tow sack
And you sent 'em back with a shove
I hear a long gone whistle on a rusty track
I got a towsack full of love

Chorus:
I got a towsack full of love, for all the time we've been apart.
I got a towsack full of postage due on my poor ole one-way
    heart.

Now you won't get a letter in the morning mail
And the mail train can whistle by my door
Gonna hang your package on a rusty nail
That I won't be needin' any more
I'm going to find me a holler where the lonesome's fine
And put a keep-out sign above
And you can stick your letters where the sun don't shine
I've had a towsack full of love.

NEVER HIT YOUR GRANDMA WITH A GREAT BIG STICK
Lyrics by Mitch Jayne

Used to stay at granny's house, back in Tennessee
Just a dear old lady, as grandmas tend to be
Cousin Buford's sling shot
Whacked her in the face
I think Buford's buried there, somewhere on the place.

Chorus:
Never hit your granny
With a great big stick
She may do the cookin'
And make you mighty sick
Granny's got a temper, boy
When you make her sore
People who make granny mad
Don't live here any more

Granny's face is wrinkled, hair as white as snow
Gentle eyes that twinkle, rosy cheeks aglow
Once a nasty neighbor pulled
Granny's silver hair
Spent a lot of idle time in intensive care

Chorus:
Never hit your granny
With a great big stick
She may do the cookin'
And make you mighty sick
Granny's got a temper, boy
When you make her sore
People who make granny mad
Don't live here any more

Listen to the Sound

"Bluegrass is like riding a wave that never breaks."

—*Mitch Jayne*

Bluegrass music posed particular problems for musicians, as its esoteric style made it difficult to pigeonhole. Bluegrass pioneers such as Bill Monroe and Ralph Stanley performed on the Grand Ole Opry stage, but they never achieved the status of a headline act. Instead, they were relegated to fill-in or back-up band status, or used primarily as an instrumental band to perform dance numbers.

Economically, bluegrass offered few incentives. The only radio airplay bluegrass appeared to receive on a regular basis was as background music for furniture sale commercials.

",Bluegrass didn't fit completely with the folk scene, and it certainly was never really part of the country music scene. Bluegrass was always a form of music that seemed to be forever standing in the wings waiting to be recognized," Mitch Jayne explained.

Bluegrass started to attract a national audience

Sweet Harmony—The Dillards turned unsuspecting
audiences on to the richness of bluegrass
music.   —*photo courtesy of the Dillards*

only after the Osborne Brothers recorded their classic
version of "Rocky Top." Suddenly, bluegrass music
began to receive more recognition and airplay time
on local radio stations.

Jayne remembers "Rocky Top" as the first bluegrass song heard on AM stations across the United
States. The song made great strides for bluegrass
music. Prior to the Osborne Brothers' hit, it was very
difficult for bluegrass musicians to find steady work
unless the act was unusual. The Dillards fell into the
unusual category, as they combined traditional and
original bluegrass tunes with sophisticated comedy.

The growing popularity of bluegrass music created a new problem for the Dillards. Dozens of bluegrass bands suddenly started popping up throughout

the country covering one anothers' songs in steady succession. As a result, it became increasingly difficult to distinguish a bluegrass band from Eminence, Missouri, from a bluegrass band from Queens, New York.

"One of the things we decided before we ever left Salem was that the band had to be unique. We sat on the back porch of my house and rehearsed and practiced songs for a year. Rodney, Dean and I started writing songs together because we felt it was extremely important that we develop and perform our own material instead of copying someone else. We wanted the band to represent the Ozark approach to bluegrass. Bluegrass music is a very mountainy type of music. If you took away the Ozark name from it folks would still recognize it as mountain music, no matter whatever set of mountains they came from. Listening to the songs playing on the radio, we could tell that everybody was already copying each other and bands were sounding very much alike. What we wanted to accomplish more than anything was to be different. I still believe that the best thing we ever did for the music was to bring our own uniqueness, whatever that is, to bluegrass," Mitch contends, reflecting on the Dillards' career.

Accompanied by a choir of crickets and cicadas and playing in the soft glow of lightening bugs, the boys practiced outside Mitch's home. When they weren't adding a new layer of callouses to their fingers, the Dillards were writing songs. Rodney developed the melodies, while Mitch used his gift for language to paint vivid tableaus of Ozark life and its people.

Mitch discovered that writing lyrics came natur-

Listen to the Sound

ally. Although he had never written a song before joining the group, he had written a great deal of poetry. He lived by the writer's rule of writing only about familiar subjects, and Mitch knew plenty of colorful characters to fill a songbook.

"We wanted to write songs which described the Ozarks and dealt with the kind of people who lived there, which we did through songs such as "Ebo Walker" and "Dooley," Mitch remembered. "When I first started writing songs, they were very simple with a beginning, middle and an end. Heck, I didn't even know what a bridge was. The songs were like poems that told a story. "The Old Home Place" is just a poem set to music where you repeat the refrain."

When the Dillards arrived in California, there were other bluegrass groups vying for gigs. While these other groups weren't starving to death, only a handful were able to rely exclusively on their musical talent to earn a living. The majority of the California-based bluegrass groups were forced to work day jobs to supplement their income. The Dillards were intent on succeeding because they had driven two thousand miles to give music their best shot, and in the words of Aunt Dollie, if they flopped they'd be a long ways from home.

"We were so fortunate to get that job on *The Andy Griffith Show*. I don't think we would have turned out to be like any of the other bluegrass groups anyway, but being on the Griffith show enabled us to ripen and to change to that whole intellectual climate that was surrounding folk music at that time," Mitch remarked.

Rodney and Mitch composed songs at a furious

pace during the group's formative days. Tunes constantly flowed through Rodney's mind, sometimes
too early in the morning to suit Mitch. Once the
group had settled in California it was not unusual
for Rodney to call Mitch at four o'clock in the morning, bubbling with excitement about a new tune that
had just popped into his head. Mitch, his mind
somewhere off in Missouri, would be groggy and
flustered, having been rudely awakened from a perfectly sound sleep and perhaps cheated out of a ri-
veting dream. Rodney would hum the melody to
Mitch, and then urge him to come up with words to
fit Rodney's concept.

At times, Mitch developed sets of lyrics around a
particular Ozark-related story that he felt a need to
tell. Rodney would then create a tune to complement
the words. On other occasions, Rodney would initi-
ate the song by composing a tune, and then chal-
lenge Mitch to write suitable lyrics to fit the mood.

"Rodney would write a tune and I would say,
'What does that make you think of?' and he would
throw me a framework and I would develop it into a
complete story. For a time there, Rodney and I were
so productive and worked so well together, it was
like we were (John) Lennon and (Paul) McCartney."

Songs rarely lay dormant. Once a song was pol-
ished shiny as a fresh apple, the Dillards would test
it out on an audience. Songs written on a Tuesday afternoon routinely debuted publicly on Wednesday or
Thursday, if a gig was scheduled.

Back Porch
Bluegrass

Jac Holzman and Jim Dickson watched in open-mouthed amazement as the Dillards recorded their debut album. What dumbfounded the record company brass was Douglas Dillard's electrifying fingers sliding skillfully up and down the banjo neck like a runaway train.

"We were in the studio recording "Banjo in the Hollow" and the president of Elektra Records just kept staring at Douglas and shook his head in awe. Here Douglas was picking this song fantastically fast and he was smoking a pipe at the same time, looking as though there was nothing to banjo picking," Dean recalled.

Critics reacted harshly to the July 1964 release of *Back Porch Bluegrass*. No one in the industry, outside a few flabbergasted executives at Elektra Records, had ever heard a banjo player pick as ferociously as Douglas Dillard. Reviewers launched scathing attacks on the band, accusing the Dillards and Elektra of artificially speeding up the recording. Incensed by the verbal assault, the band members marched to the studio to inspect the master tape. A check of the master proved that the album's speed was correct.

Critics also bemoaned the use of an echo chamber, saying it detracted from the purity of bluegrass. "Since when," one critic charged, "does a back porch have an echo chamber?"

"Well, if you've ever played on the back porch of a house located in a hollow, one thing you'll hear is a natural echo," Rodney explained, still rankled by a statement made nearly thirty years ago. "The problem with those critics was that they were from New York, and their idea of a rural experience was seeing a dead squirrel in a parking lot. You had these Yankees who wanted to find some roots, so they put on blue shirts and vests and called themselves the "Something Valley Boys" without ever having grown up in the concept. They wanted to take on the ambience of country people and then make judgements on their music."

Rodney adamantly refuses to listen to *Back Porch Bluegrass*. Chosen to serve as the band's lead vocalist, on the album, Rodney felt unprepared for the role.

"I hated *Back Porch Bluegrass* when I first heard it, and to this day I will not play the album. I simply wasn't ready to be a lead vocalist and I didn't like the way my voice was recorded. Everybody else in the group performed well, but I didn't like my part," he said.

Dean understands Rodney's sentiments on the album. Although, he does not judge the work as harshly as Rodney, Dean agrees that the recording represents a period when the band members were still learning the ropes.

"Watching the Andy Griffith reruns, I can tell

how my mandolin playing improved from our first episode to our second appearance even though they were filmed only a matter of months apart. We were either playing at clubs or rehearsing every day, and when you do that you are going to naturally improve," Dean said.

The debut album was appropriately named, as many of the songs had been composed on the back porch of Mitch's home in Salem. *Back Porch Bluegrass* included three classic banjo instrumentals penned by Douglas Dillard: "Banjo in the Hollow," "Hickory Hollow" and "Doug's Tune." The album also featured two songs which have since become bluegrass standards: "The Old Home Place," written by Dean and Mitch, and "Dooley," composed by Rodney and Mitch.

"Dooley" evolved inside The Showboat, a Los Angeles night spot owned by the Everly Brothers, who envisioned the club as offering a diverse mix of entertainment each night. Patrons could choose from folk, jazz, and rock, simply by moving from room to room.

All the performers shared a communal dressing room and could hear each other rehearse their songs. As the Dillards prepared for the evening's performance, the singing of an old spiritual coming from a few dressing stalls over caught their attention. Rodney commented to Mitch that if the tune was turned around a bit and new words developed, they could have a nice bluegrass song. Later that evening, after their show, Mitch penned the words to "Dooley" and Rodney developed the tune.

"I'd been wanting to write a song about moonshine for a long time," Mitch recalled. "Everyone that came backstage after shows loved to talk to us about moonshine. They'd ask what it was like, and had we ever drunk any before. We'd describe it to them and explain to them that moonshine wasn't a social drink in the Ozarks. If you drank too much of moonshine, you had to hold onto the grass in order to lean against the ground."

Webb and Jayne's composition "The Old Home Place," reflects on the plight of displaced farmers. Called by the lure of city life and a better-paying job, the farmer leaves home only to realize his love is the family homestead. When he attempts to return home, he discovers that it is too late to reclaim his past life.

> *What have they done with the old home place,*
> *Why did they tear it down.*
> *And why did I leave the plow in the fields*
> *And look for a job in the town?*

"Dean and I wrote "The Old Home Place" in one afternoon," Mitch explained. "We were talking, and I asked Dean 'Do you suppose we'll get terrible homesick out there? And what would happen if we were to come back and this house wouldn't be here any more?" As it turns out, that did happen. The people who bought my house after we left burned it down, and there was no old home place to come back to."

A song destined to create quite a stir for the Dillards was "Duelin Banjo," which appeared on the group's debut album. Dean and Douglas are credited with the arrangement, which features an escalating duel between Dean's mandolin and Douglas' frenetic banjo picking. The song was immensely popular among Dillards fans. Douglas had originally heard it in the 1950s, when a different arrangement was released by Don Reno and Arthur Smith. The 1955 version was called "Feuding Banjos," and featured a battle between a tenor banjo and a five-string. Carl Story recorded the tune two years later as "Mocking Banjo."

The most famous arrangement came nearly ten years later with the film *Deliverance*. Eric Weissberg, who ironically had been in the Elektra Records studio when the Dillards originally cut "Duelin' Banjo," released a new arrangement with guitarist Steve Mandell. The duo changed the title slightly, adding the letter "g" to the end of "Duelin" and making "banjo" plural, thus changing it to "Dueling Banjos." The popularity of the movie rekindled interest in the song, which also inspired Arthur Smith to file a multi million dollar lawsuit against the Dillards for stealing his song.

Late one evening, a sheriff's deputy banged on Douglas' door and handed the musician a summons. Douglas read the official-looking piece of paper while the deputy looked on somberly. Instead of becoming enraged, Douglas surprised the law officer by erupting in laughter. The band eventually hired a musicologist to research the origin of the song, and discovered that it went back to an 1889 tune entitled "Banjo Reel." The suit against the Dillards was dismissed, much to the band's relief.

The Dillards
Live . . .
Almost

Mitch Jayne joined the Dillards because it provided him the perfect opportunity to shine in public doing what he did best, spinning yarns and telling tales about the people of the Ozarks. The only problem was that Douglas was an exceptional banjo picker, and Mitch needed to learn another instrument if he was going to contribute musically.

"I didn't learn to play the bass until just right before the band got ready to go out on the road. When I decided that I wanted to be a member of the Dillards the only instrument we needed was a bass, so Rodney, Dean and Douglas taught me how to play. Those guys could play almost anything," Mitch explained. "Playing the bass was always very secondary for me. I was never all that wonderful of a player. I was adequate, and that came from working under the tutelage of Rodney Dillard. When you performed with Rodney, you had to be more than adequate if you wanted to keep up and add anything to the band."

Rodney, Mitch went on, was the band's musical driver. A perfectionist, Rodney took great pains to ensure that every aspect of each performance was the best possible. His desire for perfection included not only the music, but the stories Mitch would tell. Mitch's primary job was to weave stories, get laughs, and make the audience feel comfortable with the band.

The group's follow-up album, *The Dillards Live . . . Almost,* was released by Elektra Records in November 1964. The album was recorded live during a three-night engagement at The Mecca, a popular Los Angeles folk music club, and showcased Mitch's comic wit. Live albums proved tricky, as a perfectly performed song or comedy routine could be ruined in a heartbeat by the sound of a dropped beer pitcher, a cough, an argument, or an ill-timed telephone call. Despite the difficulties, Dickson performed a masterful piece of editing and created a memorable album which accurately captured the essence of the original Dillards. The album is treasured by Dillards fans and collectors and is nearly impossible to locate, according to Douglas. The following is an excerpt in which Mitch attempts to break the ice by telling the audience about the group's upbringing.

"This song is a folk song that you've probably heard done lots of times before. It's about a dog and the name of the song is 'Old Blue.' Rodney does a pretty good job of singing this, but I would like to say one thing. He may not sing it the way you are used to it, because we didn't know it was done any other way except ours until last year, when we heard Joan Baez sing this at a festival we played at. She had everybody crying and frothing at the mouth. Rodney bit Pete Seeger on the leg. It was just a real emotional and moving experience about this old dog. This song we do a lot different, and I think it is be-

cause we've got a little different attitude about dogs down home. I know we've got a lot different attitude about dogs than they do in Los Angeles, because we don't shave them up in little balls like they do in Beverly Hills and dye them lavender and stuff. You may not know this, but we don't put rhinestone collars on them too much either. You know, if there was a rhinestone collar to spare around the house, it went on mommy.

"Dogs are a status symbol down home. You need four or five of them in the summertime, laying out there in the front yard scratching for the tourists and all. What I started to tell you, though, I think the real reason we do this song so much different is that we've got privies down home. I don't know if you know what those are. If not, then lotsa luck. They are a little pine shed which usually sits about a hundred yards out behind the house in the Ozarks, which in the winter time is of course a hundred yards too far; but in the summer time it's about a hundred yards too near. It's like everything else, you have to have sort of a compromise there.

"The thing is that people run fox hounds down there. Well a fox hound, I don't know if you know what that is either, but these are hounds that run in packs of ten or twenty and they don't have any sense, they're just like, you know, (nods in the direction of Rodney). They won't just run all night, they'll run for a week until finally their paws give out. They get starved to death, and cold, and especially in the winter they'll lay up in the first place they find that is out of the wind, which if you've left the door open is your privy.

"You talk about something that will shake your day up. This has happened to all of us at different times. You have to get up, maybe in the middle of a cold winter night, with a little skiff of snow on the ground, and everything outside is of course slicker than deer guts on a door knob. You have to go out there for some reason or another . . . well, let me put it this way. If you're up at that time of the morning and in that kind of weather, it's prob-

ably an emergency kind of thing with you. You get out there to the privy finally, through maybe five or six inches of snow, and you open the door and here is this big blue tick hound of somebody's curled up in there going (loud snore) like he built it. I'll tell you the long and short of it, I figure that anybody who has been growled out of their own privy five or six times in the winter is not going to sing 'Old Blue' like Joan Baez does."

Comedy aside, the album claims another distinction as the first record to contain a bluegrass version of a Bob Dylan tune. Mitch routinely poked a bit of fun at Dylan's expense each time he introduced the song. Once the joke nearly backfired, Douglas gleefully recalled.

"One night at The Troubadour we did a Bob Dylan song, "Walking Down the Line." Now, Mitch would always have a few words to say about each song that we played. He introduced this song and complimented Dylan on writing such great stuff, but added that Dylan's only problem was that he sang with a voice that sounded like a dog with its leg caught in barbed wire. As soon as the words were out of his mouth, we realized that Bob Dylan was seated there in the front row. Fortunately, he had a good sense of humor and just laughed," Douglas recalled with a cackle of laughter himself.

"Bob had been to see several of our shows, and we were friends. He even taught my oldest daughter some licks on the guitar, so we knew him well," Mitch added. "When I saw him sitting there I knew that he wouldn't get mad, but it was embarrassing. Of course, Rodney was strangling in laughter."

The Dillards Live . . . Almost includes Dillards gems such as "I'll Never See My Home Again," "The

Whole World 'Round," and the classic "There is a Time." Douglas' lightening fingers stretch the boundaries of credulity in "Bucking Mule," where his Gibson banjo manages to assume the familiar braying sound of an annoyed mule.

"There Is A Time" ranks as one of Mitch's favorite songs. Mitch wrote the lyrics first, and Rodney followed with the tune. The entire song just took two days to complete. "There Is A Time" perfectly reflected the Dillards' stage of development. When Mitch wrote the song on the back porch of his home in Salem they were all young, and it was time for the Dillards to go wandering like the Scarecrow, the Cowardly Lion and the Tin Woodsman.

Vanguard Records released *There Is A Time* in 1991 which contains six cuts from the live album. With the exception of Mitch's band member introduction, none of the group's comic interaction was captured on the compilation recording, much to the Dillards' disappointment.

Pickin'
and
Fiddlin'

Pickin' and Fiddlin', the band's third and nearly their last offering from Elektra, was released in February 1965 and paid tribute to the Dillards' musical heritage. *Pickin' and Fiddlin'* was indeed a dramatic departure from the Dillards' previous efforts, as the fiddle was prominently emphasized in tunes such as "Hamilton County Breakdown" and "Paddy on the Turnpike."

The album featured an addition to the band—fiddler Byron Berline, who had met the Dillards at a college concert in Norman, Oklahoma. After the Dillards' first show, Berline came backstage with his fiddle case in hand. A big, likeable fella, Berline hit it off instantly with the Dillards, and within a matter of minutes he had his fiddle out and was jamming with the band. The Dillards were so impressed that they invited him join them onstage for the second show. Douglas and Rodney were both intrigued by Berline's talent.

Pickin' and Fiddlin' represented the Dillards' attempt to smooth the ruffled feathers of bluegrass purists. The commercial success of the band, coupled with the innovative style in which the Dillards presented bluegrass music, had offended the old guard. Yet, it was their very original and imaginative techniques that was rekindling excitement in the music and attracting first-time listeners to bluegrass. Rodney lamented that it seemed as though the purists actually preferred that the music remain hidden in the shadows of obscurity.

"Their attitude seemed to be that if a group was commercially successful, then you couldn't be a purist. It was like they wanted to squirrel away the music and keep it to themselves like a groundhog," he said.

The Dillards owed Elektra one final album. The group decided to demonstrate to the bluegrass elite that the Dillards could play the old-fashion style. Rodney approached Elektra Records about the possibility of doing an instrumental album, and received the go-ahead. Once project approval was granted, the Dillards knew Berline was the right person to join the group on fiddle. They went a step further by convincing Ralph Rinzler to write the album notes for *Pickin' and Fiddlin'*. Rinzler is credited with discovering Bill Monroe and Doc Watson, and his stamp of approval would carry a great weight on the album's acceptance.

Pickin' and Fiddlin', an esoteric mix of strictly instrumental banjo and fiddle tunes was well received by the bluegrass powers. Mitch and Douglas thoroughly enjoyed the uniqueness of the album.

"Nobody knew where the music was going at the time," Mitch recalled. "The only thing that had happened since the folk wave was the Beatles. The Beatles were the biggest thing that ever happened in this country musically. Well, not every record company could get a group like the Beatles, or even a good imitation, so they went scrambling to find something else. Elektra was very open to experimenting at the time, and agreed to let us do the album. I was very proud of the fiddle album and how well Byron performed with us. He showed that the fiddle is part of bluegrass music."

The Dillards constantly rattled the cages of bluegrass purists with their progressive style. They experimented with electric instruments and occasionally added drums to the mix. An example of the latter came in 1965, when they added drummer Dewey Martin to the band for a road trip. The Dillards were beginning a summer tour and wanted to use this time to experiment with different sounds. Martin, an unkown drummer, was searching for work, and the band hired him for the tour.

"You have to remember, we weren't playing any bluegrass festivals," Rodney explained. "We were doing the rock and roll circuit with groups like Sam the Sham, Mitch Ryder and the Detroit Wheels, and the Byrds. When we added Dewey to the band, it was like we were grinding up sacred cows for hamburgers."

Back home in Los Angeles following the tour, Rodney was approached by Stephen Stills, who was rehearsing at the nearby Rainbow Music Hall. Stills was involved in the formation of a new group, and they were in dire need of an accomplished drummer. Rodney introduced Stills to Martin, and the two hit it off well. They teamed with future legend Neil Young to form Buffalo Springfield.

By this time, the Dillards had left the Elektra label and signed a contract with Capitol Records. The band languished at Capitol; they were repeatedly bumped from one producer to another, and never found any continuity. The Dillards cut several sides toward creating an album but never finished the project. The final straw came when the Dillards were called into an executive board meeting. One of the executives explained that his nephew had written a song, "The Gunslinger's Union," which he thought would be a perfect tune for the Dillards to record.

"It was the worst thing we had ever heard. We finally just got up and left," Rodney recalled.

Elektra welcomed the Dillards' return, and the stage was set for the band's most celebrated release.

Wheatstraw Suite

A feeling of restlessness began creeping in on Rodney as the 1960s neared a close. *Back Porch Bluegrass, The Dillards Live . . . Almost* and *Pickin' and Fiddlin'* had given the band a core of followers, but the musical world was changing. The trumpet player hidden inside Rodney was yearning to explore different venues, much to the displeasure of his older brother.

"I felt extremely limited by bluegrass, and I was ready for a radical change. *Wheatstraw Suite* was a departure from the traditional Dillards music," Rodney said.

The concept for *Wheatstraw Suite* developed gradually in 1967-68. Rodney's ambition was to inject a completely unique texture and flavor into the Dillards' music. This would include full orchestration, with pedal steel, stringed instruments, drums, and multi-track recording technology. This represented a dramatic shift from the banjo-heavy songs contained in the band's three previous releases. He attempted to convey this new idea to the band and encountered heavy resistance from Douglas.

"Douglas didn't want to change the rhythm of the music, and I could understand his feelings," Rodney said. "Douglas is a banjo picker and a bluegrass player. That is what he does and it is what he loves. There is no banjo player in the world better than Douglas. The problem was that I simply could not live, breathe, and sleep bluegrass music—it's just not in me. Bluegrass is a wonderful thing and I'm glad we have it to enjoy. Bluegrass represents my roots and it gave me my start, but at the time, I wanted to explore other musical styles."

Douglas argued vehemently against the change, but Dean and Mitch sided with Rodney. After a bitter argument one day, Douglas announced that he was quitting the band and walked out the door.

Douglas accepted an offer to accompany the Byrds on an European tour. When creative differences convinced Gene Clark to leave the Byrds, he and Douglas teamed up to form The Dillard and Clark Expedition. The pair worked together for three years and recorded two albums, *The Fantastic Expedition of Dillard and Clark* and *Through the Morning, Through the Night*, both on the A&M label. Ironically, when Douglas teamed up with Gene Clark to form The Dillard and Clark Expedition, the music featured on the group's two albums leaned more toward folk and country music than traditional bluegrass.

Back at Elektra, even Rodney suffered occasional pangs of uncertainty prior to the release of *Wheatstraw Suite*. The remaining band members recognized the time for change had arrived, but bluegrass music and the comic routines had become the group's security blanket. The Dillards were earning a comfortable living, and changing the formula meant running the risk of failure. Conversely, the British Invasion had seriously damaged interest in folk and bluegrass music, and it was evident that the musical world was in a state of transition.

"We all agreed that it was either adapt or perish," Dean recalled. "When we started out, we all wore buckskins and moccasins and played old songs, or original songs that sounded like old songs. We even had a rule that you couldn't wear jewelry on stage, not even a watch, unless it was a pocket watch. Well, eventually you paint yourself in a corner, as it becomes more difficult to come up with fresh songs that sound like the old folk songs. The first albums we did are good, but you can't record the same album over and over. You've got to progress. It's like sending a child to school. There is a lot of excitement in a child entering the first grade, but you don't want the child to stay in the first grade forever."

The shift in the musical culture presented fresh opportunities for bands. Performers took advantage of this progressive period by becoming more daring and experimental. The Dillards were no different. Rodney relates the Dillards experience to a similar one described to him by Earl Scruggs. Scruggs once told Rodney that in the early stages of his career he simply played the banjo and wasn't constrained by the rules of being categorized. The rigidity of bluegrass soured Rodney, as he despised the concept that bluegrass should be limited to a classic form and stance.

"When you are afraid of breaking tradition, you are creating your own limitations," Rodney said. "Breaking tradition means that you are actually creating a **new** tradition. If you go into a project with fear of failure, then you can never jump that ditch."

Herb Pedersen was brought in, at Dean's suggestion, to replace Douglas on the banjo and provide vocal help. Dean had heard Pedersen during the group's early days in Los Angeles; He also knew that Pedersen occasionally substituted for Earl Scruggs.

"I figured that if Earl Scruggs thought Herb was good enough to sub for him, that he had to be pretty good. Herb was back in Nashville, so I called him, and he was eager to join the group," Dean said.

Pedersen's arrival added a new dimension to the band's sound, as his tenor voice provided a strong third harmony that the band had previously lacked. Supplementing the original band were Buddy Emmons on pedal steel guitar, Joe Osborn on the electric bass, and drummers Toxey French and Jimmy Gordon.

The two brothers had received solo offers prior to

The Dillards with their newest member, Herb Pedersen (back row, right), promote the release of their classic *Wheatstraw Suite* album on *The Joey Bishop Show*. —*photo courtesy of the Dillards*

Douglas' departure. Rodney had been approached by CBS about the possibility of performing in a situation comedy revolving around two piano movers. Douglas had received offers to play on the *Bonnie and Clyde* soundtrack album. Rodney and Douglas had earlier provided musical accompaniment on the actual movie soundtrack. Rodney and Douglas declined such solo offers, fearing that such individual excursions might disrupt the band's harmony. Now, soured by the band's sudden division, Rodney secretly decided that *Wheatstraw Suite* would be his final album.

"I was going to get out of the business. At the time there were other venues opening up to me, but when the album was released it made such an impact that it turned things around for the band. We suddenly found ourselves playing this new sound that people were listening to with a great deal of interest."

Magazine critics such as those at *Rolling Stone* praised *Wheatstraw Suite*. The final line in the *Rolling Stone* review sums up the album by stating, "*Wheatstraw Suite* is a treat." A decade later, the album continued to stand as a milestone in the history of folk and country-rock music. The *Rolling Stone Record Guide* noted that the "album is a brilliant rush of fierce playing and beautifully precise vocal harmonies with several excellent originals ("Nobody Knows," "Listen to the Sound"), and covers of the Beatles "I've Just Seen a Face."

Perhaps even more pleasing were the accolades expressed by the band's peers. Blood, Sweat and Tears, the Byrds, and Linda Ronstadt loved the album's combination of bluegrass harmonies and a rock and roll feel. The sound of *Wheatstraw Suite* was neither country nor bluegrass—it was uniquely the Dillards. Multi-track recording enabled the band to duplicate versions of the harmony parts and blend them together for a smoother sound. This vocal style, used later by Crosby, Stills and Nash and the Eagles, would eventually be tabbed as the "West Coast Sound."

"Before *Wheatstraw Suite*, the instrumental was our long suit. When Herb joined the band and we did *Wheatstraw Suite*, we began to concentrate more on vocals. When that record came out it was one of our best albums," Dean contends. *Wheatstraw Suite* was Dillard music. It is hard to call it anything else."

Years later, music critics recognized the Dillards as among the pioneers of country rock. *Wheatstraw Suite* provided the musical inspiration for groups such as Crosby, Stills and Nash and the Eagles. Contained in the liner notes of the *Common Threads* compact disc is a note by Don Henley, a founding member of the Eagles, which credits the Dillards as influencing the sound of the Eagles.

"The European press acknowledges the Dillards impact on country rock even more," Rodney explained. "While we were performing in Europe, someone showed us the Family Tree of Country Rock. The roots start with the Dillards and then the Flying Burrito Brothers."

Rodney considers *Wheatstraw Suite* as his finest piece of work.

"*Wheatstraw Suite* represents a turning point for me and the band. I was finally able to express myself musically."

"She Sang Hymns Out Of Tune" marked the first song the Dillards ever recorded with a full orchestra. Using a forty-piece orchestra was Rodney's idea, and is considered by Mitch as being one of the finest pieces of work ever produced by the Dillards.

"She Sang Hymns Out of Tune" is a fanciful little song that starts softly with Herb's banjo solo and then builds gradually. Herb sang that song like a bird on that album," Mitch said. "At the end of the first verse this whole flock of violins comes in, and suddenly we are surrounded by all this music. At the end of the next verse all of the woodwinds come in, and then the brass. We were all sitting there in this studio just dumbfounded by this beautiful sound. We were never the same people after that experience. It changed us all in ways like, 'Did I give birth to **that**?'"

Along with original compositions, *Wheatstraw Suite* contained the first Beatles songs ("I've Just Seen A Face") recorded in bluegrass style. Mitch remarked that he was constantly amazed by Rodney's ability to spot the bluegrass potential of songs heard on the radio.

"Rodney had an ear for things that were translatable," Mitch said. "He would often double or quadruple the beat in his mind. Rodney was always opening new doors to the group. Playing Beatle tunes could wear a bluegrass bass-fiddler to death. We were doubling the beat the Beatles played and they were already singing their songs very briskly. But it was almost like a waltz time compared to the way the Dillards played."

The musical diversity of *Back Porch Bluegrass*, *Pickin' and Fiddlin'*, and *Wheatstraw Suite* opened new venues to bluegrass performers who followed the Dillards. No longer could bluegrass music simply be confined to a standard acoustic format of mandolin, bass, banjo and guitar. Bluegrass could be played in the hot licks fiddle style of Byron Berline, or with a forty-piece orchestra. Performers were now limited only by their own imaginations, and the Dillards had successfully jumped that ditch.

Mitch once remarked that if Rodney Dillard was convinced that a song required the use of a herd of elephants, he would hire elephants and try them out for at least that one song. The elephants might prove flat, but Rodney would never be afraid to experiment with something new. An example of this is found in the song "Music is Music," which is contained on the *Tribute to the American Duck* album. The entire chorus is sung in a Polynesian dialect.

The following represents a partial compilation of favorite song lyrics composed by the Dillards. When possible, the origin of the song is provided.

DOOLEY

Mitch Jayne and Rodney Dillard
Lansdowne-Winston Music Publishers, ©1963

One of the things we soon discovered about "audiences" was that they loved any references to moonshine. Rodney and I wrote "Dooley" in the early part of our career. I taught one of Dooley's daughters in school. They were the type of girls that had they been hogs you would have said "ship 'em."   —*Mitch Jayne*

Dooley was a good old man he lived below the mill.
Dooley had two daughters and a forty gallon still.
One gal watched the boiler, the other watched the spout,
and Mama corked the bottles when old Dooley fetched
    them out.

Chorus:
Dooley, slippin' up the holler, Dooley, tryin' to make
    a dollar.
Dooley, give me a swaller and I'll pay you back some day

The revenuers came for him, a-slippin' thru the woods.
Dooley kept behind them all and never lost his goods.
Dooley was a trader when into town he come,
Sugar by the bushel and molasses by the ton.

Chorus:
I remember very well the day old Dooley died,
The women folk looked sorry and the men stood 'round
    and cried
Now Dooley's on the mountain, he lies there all alone,
They put a jug beside him and a barrel for a stone.

Chorus:

THE OLD HOME PLACE

Mitch Jayne and Dean Webb
Lansdowne-Winston Music Publishers, ©1963

"The Old Home Place" was, in a way, a form of catharsis. Dean and I were already planning about what would happen if we didn't make it in California, or if we did succeed only to find that it wasn't worth it and we came home. It is sort of a Dorothy and the Wizard of Oz-type song, where the character discovers that what was really important to him was in his backyard in the first place. This song seemed like such an apt description of the Dillards to me. We left Missouri for Hollywood to see the Wizard, and what I realized later was that what I wanted out of that whole thing was to go back home and write.   —Mitch Jayne

It's been ten long years since I left my home
In the hollow where I was born.
Where the cool fall nights make the wood smoke rise
And a fox hunter blew his horn.

Chorus:
What have they done to the old home place
Why did they tear it down.
And why did I leave the plow in the field
And look for a job in the town.

I fell in love with a girl in the town.
I thought that she would be true.
I ran away to Charlottesville.
And worked in a sawmill crew.

Chorus:
Well, the girl ran off with somebody else;
The taverns took all my pay.
And here I stand where the old home stood
Before they took it away.

Chorus:
Now the geese fly south and the cold wind moans
As I stand here and hang my head.
I've lost my love, I've lost my home
And now I wish that I was dead.

Chorus:

THE WHOLE WORLD 'ROUND

Mitchell Jayne and Joe Stuart
Lansdowne-Winston Music Publishers, ©1963

*We were playing a festival one time, and Joe Stuart invited me
back to his hotel room one night after the show. Joe got his fiddle
out from under the bed and said, "I've got this old tune—you
might just like to write words to this thing. I don't know why it
sticks to me." As he played the tune, I was making up words to
the chorus. It was one of those kind of magical things.*

—Mitch Jayne

I heard my neighbor's rooster crow early in the day
I heard his ax beyond the hill and now I'm bound away

For some men love the city life
Some men crave the town
But I'll be bound for the lonesome woods
Where I can settle down.

Chorus:
Fiddle and a bow and firelight's glow
You can hear that lonesome sound
I'll leave behind my troublin' mind
And go the whole world 'round.

The red squirrel leaves when the grey squirrel comes
The eagles nest alone
A hundred miles from a wagon track
Is where I'll build my home.

Chorus:
I see the old man whittlin' wood
I see the streets of town
I packed my goods for the Arkansas woods,
And there I'll settle down.

Chorus:

NOBODY KNOWS

Mitch Jayne and Rodney Dillard
Lansdowne-Winston Music Publishers, ©1965

We were in Los Angeles, and it struck me funny that all the guys were constantly falling in and out of love. When they fell in love it was a head-over-heels thing. They would forget the words to songs, or forget about a gig, things they would have never done in other circumstances. The song is about how nobody can explain why love does the things to you, or why love goes away.

—*Mitch Jayne*

Nobody knows, nobody ever knows.
No one ever knows why things won't stay the same.
She's in love with you,
And you know you love her too,
There will come a time when she won't know your name.

There's a lot of things that die
Every time a day goes by,
There's a lot things that people can't explain.
You can be in love today
Meaning every word you say.
Knowing when tomorrow comes the words you say,
Will be a lie.

Nobody knows, nobody ever knows,
No one ever knows why love must go away;
We play a game,
Never really know the name,
Never really understand the game we play.
She's in love you,
And you know you love her too,
There will come a time when she won't know your name.

THERE IS A TIME

Rodney Dillard and Mitch Jayne
Lansdowne-Winston Music Publishers, ©1964

Seasons are something all people have in common. A friend wrote me once and said he wanted the words to "There Is A Time" read at his funeral. What had caught him were the four steps of life: the time to go roaming, the time to find love, the time to appreciate the harvest of your life, and the time to sleep.

—*Mitch Jayne*

There is a time for love and laughter
The days will pass like summer storms
The winter wind will follow after
But there is love and love is warm.

Chorus:
There is a time for us to wander
When time is young and so are we.
The woods are greener over yonder
The path is new, the world is free.

There is a time when leaves are falling.
The woods are grey, the paths are old.
The snow will come when geese are calling.
You need a fire against the cold.

Chorus:
So do your roaming in the spring-time,
And find your love in the summer sun,
The frost will come and bring the harvest,
And you can sleep when the day is done.

Chorus:

EBO WALKER

Mitch Jayne and Rodney Dillard
Lansdowne-Winston Music Publishers, ©1964

"Ebo Walker" came from half a dozen people who were Ebo Walker-type of characters. Ebo was the kind of guy who never did a thing in his life except grow ginseng or let his wife support him by working in the shoe factory. If he didn't dig roots to make a living, he hunted out of season, drank, and played the fiddle, usually in that order. "Ebo Walker" started out as a very simple story, but Rodney, Douglas, Dean, and I would enlarge on it all the time until finally we would do a full ten-minute routine on Ebo.
                                                    —*Mitch Jayne*

Ebo Walker was a good ole man. (in harmony)

Ebo Walker was born in Kentucky
And raised by his daddy on a hillside farm
He took up fiddle playing just for fun.
That's the last work that Ebo Walker done.

Ebo Walker was a good ole man.
Ebo Walker was a good ole man.

Chorus:
Now, Ebo Walker, he left Kentucky
Cause Ebo's daddy said, durn your hide.
You won't plant corn, you won't make hay
Just sit on the porch and play that thing all day.

Now, Ebo Walker walked thru the mountains
With his fiddle in his sack
And his shoes in his hand.
He fiddled a tune for the folks he met,
Just to fill his belly and keep his whistle wet.

Ebo Walker was a good ole man.
Ebo Walker was a good ole man.

Chorus:
Now, Ebo Walker he walked and he fiddled.
And he fiddled and he walked
And he drank till he died.
But I've heard tell when the wind is down.
And the moon shines bright,
And the leaves turn brown.
You can hear old Ebo fiddlin' all aroun'.

Ebo Walker was a good ole man (harmony)
Ebo Walker was a good ole man (harmony)

LISTEN TO THE SOUND
Herb Pedersen and Mitch Jayne
Nipper Music Company, ©1968

I like "Listen to the Sound" awfully well. Rodney and I wrote that at a time when we realized that people were pushing the envelope as hard as they could with bluegrass. They were trying to make it things that it wasn't. If there was ever a theme that Rodney and I had in common that sewed our separate languages together, it was 'don't pay any attention to the rules; listen to the sound.' It is the music that has the magic in it. It's not how we dress, or what we say, or how much or little we entertain. The main thing is listen to the sound, and see what it does to you.

—Mitch Jayne

You were born by the rollin' ocean,
I was born by the mountains green,
Sing to the wind and the wind will tell you
All of the things the wind has seen.

Chorus:
Listen to the sound, listen to the sound
Listen to the sound that the wind brought down;
Listen to the old time sound of the fiddle,
Telling of a place you never have found.

Listen to the tin can highway hummin'
Listen to the plow in the new green ground.
Hear the sound of a freight train comin'
There could be a place you never have found.

We were born by different highways,
That's the difference in our ways.
You can hear a sound of far-off places,
Echoes of a song in other days.

You were born by the rollin' ocean
I was born in the mountains green.
Sing to the wind and the wind will tell you
All of the things you never have seen.

Chorus:
Listen to the sound, listen to the sound
Listen to the sound that the wind brought down;
Listen to the old time sound of the fiddle,
Telling of a place you never have found.

HEY BOYS
Rodney Dillard, Mitch Jayne, Dean Webb
and Herb Pedersen
Nipper Music Company, ©1968

"Hey Boys" is one of my favorite songs, as it describes the atti-
tude and neatness of Ozark people. Ozark people are satisfied with
where they are and what they do. They are content to sit and wat-
ch life go by, and spit every now and then in the fireplace. While
the rest of the world is busy ranting and roaring, Ozark people
kinda watch it all go by while they sit on the side of the mountain.
I heard Douglas playing this old fiddle tune once and I remem-
bered this one line, 'another little drink won't do us any harm.'
That sounded like a neat philosophical phrase and I built the song
around it.   *—Mitch Jayne*

When I was a young man I lived along the Merimac,
Washed in the river when the water ran clean
Waited for the day, I could buy me a Cadillac,
And see a lot of things that I never had seen.

Worked in the city and I got a little older
And I got a little smarter and I learned good sense.
Went back home and I married me a woman.
Got a corn-land bottom and a barbed-wire fence.

Chorus:
Hey boys, I think I'm getting old,
Sitting by the fire when the weather gets cold
Don't care, down around the farm
And another little drink won't do us any harm.

Hard times, made a little moonshine,
Never done that in my life before
Kept up with the news in the wintertime
Sittin' on a barrel in the country store.

Chorus:

Rare back, talk about your politics,
Fight about religion and worry about war.
I'll set, a-spittin' in the fireplace
Pour a little cider if your throat gets sore.

Chorus:

I'LL NEVER SEE MY HOME AGAIN
Mitch Jayne and Rodney Dillard
Lansdowne-Winston Music Publishers, ©1964

In the hollow where the pines are standing tall
In the shadows where the woods are dark and still
To a warped and weathered shack, my mind keeps
    turnin' back
To my old mountain home on the hill.

Chorus:
Oh I left it in the springtime when the flowers were
    in bloom
And I told the folks I'd see them in the fall
But the road keeps stretching onward from the cradle to
    the tomb
And I guess I'll never see my folks at all.

I can hear the geese a-cryin in the sky.
And see the dry leaves blowin' in the lane.
I miss the wood fire on a cold and rainy night
And the trees a-scratchin' at my window pane.

Chorus:
As the years go by and seasons pass away.
The homeplace keeps returning to my mind.
I'd give a lot to see that place so dear to me
That hollow in the woods I left behind.

Chorus: (with change)
Oh I left it in the spring-time when the flowers were
    in bloom
And all the birds were singing in the glen.
But the roads keeps stretching onward from the cradle to
    the tomb.
And I guess I'll never see my home again.

IN OUR TIME
Rodney Dillard and Mitch Jayne
Nipper Music Company, ©1968

*We wrote this song during a period of time when we wanted to do
something different. We wanted to give it a bluegrass feel, but we
wanted it to be different than traditional bluegrass.*
—Rodney Dillard

In the ashes of a dying love a new one has to grow.
In the footprints of another day our footsteps have to go.
And the words that we've forgotten turn to memories
    that rhyme.
In our time.

In the yellow woods of yesterday the future will be born.
And the hunting hounds remembering will answer to
    the horn.
Like the time of our beginnings, you will see the morning
    shine,
In our time.

Though the ship is caught in silence, and the wind of time
    is past.
And the rusty bells of yesterday, are silent on the mast.
We can catch the wind of morning, and again the bells
    will chime.
In our time.

Over battlefields of yesterday, tomorrow has to come.
Though the drummer is forgotten, we will recognize
    his drum.
In the faces of the children we will see tomorrow shine.
In our time.

THE BIGGEST WHATEVER
Rodney Dillard and Bill Martin
Yard Dog Music/Nipper Music Company, ©1969

Bill Martin and I wrote this song together. When I was growing up in Salem, there were several stories of Bigfoot sightings in the area. We decided to write a spoof on those sightings. All the characters mentioned in the song were actually real people from my home town. Years later Bill went on to write the movie Harry and the Hendersons, *so who knows, perhaps "The Biggest Whatever" helped spawn* Harry and the Hendersons.   —*Rodney Dillard.*

It was Dobro Wiggins while returning a jam jar to Bessie
    May Hooden Phyle's place.
About a mile outa town on the West Plains road, he dis-
    appeared without a trace.
They discovered his teeth when the county police made an
    investigation of the case.
And Cousin Belle Simmons said that Sheriff Corb Pryor had
    the strangest look on his face.
It was the biggest whatever that anybody ever saw.
It was covered with fur and came a rollin' in from Arkansas.
It was forty feet high a gleam in its eye and a big purple
    patch on its craw,
It was the biggest whatever that anybody ever saw.

I saw old man Hutzell who's a hundred and four
Yesterday, at Ida Jadwin's house;
He said it's much bigger now than when it carried off my cow.
But it's not enough to worry about.
It was the biggest whatever that anybody ever saw.
It was covered with fur and came a rollin' in from Arkansas.
It was forty feet high a gleam in its eye and a big purple
    patch on its craw,
It was the biggest whatever that anybody ever saw.

He said back before the war there was a whole lot more
But they never came this far south;
He said I don't mind seein' one from time to time
But I hope it ain't its regular route.
It was the biggest whatever that anybody ever saw.
It was covered with fur and came a rollin' in from Arkansas.

It was forty feet high a gleam in its eye and a big purple
    patch on its craw,
It was the biggest whatever that anybody ever saw.

DARLIN BOYS
Mitch Jayne, Rodney Dillard, Herb Pedersen
Full Sail Music, ©1990

*Suddenly we realized that we had done all those television shows
and had never mentioned the Darling boys in any of our songs. We
wrote and recorded the song on a whim. Receiving a Grammy nomination for that song was the furthest thing from my mind.*
—Mitch Jayne

(Voice of Briscoe Darling: "All right boys, a one and a two
    and a one and a two")

Well up on the middle of the mountain side
Where the red and the grey squirrels play.
And the sound of the fiddle when the old men died
Was to carry the souls away.
And some folks hammered on the steel all day
And some put a furrow in the ground.
But nobody did it like the Darlin boys
When the fiddle and the bow came down
When the fiddle and the bow came down.

Chorus:
Oh, the Darlin boys they all dressed funny.
And the Darlin boys they talked real slow.
But nobody did it like the Darlin boys,
When it came to the old banjo,
When it came to the old banjo.

Well, down in the middle of a one horse town
Where the steeples stand up high.
They'd paid by the gallon when the boys came down
The Mayberry town was dry.
Well the Darlin boys had traps on the river
And the Darlin boys made shine in the night.
Nobody did like the Darlin boys
When the time of the moon was right,

When the time of the moon was right.

Oh, the Darlin boys they all dressed funny.
And the Darlin boys they talked real slow.
But nobody did it like the Darlin boys,
When it came to the old banjo,
When it came to the old banjo.

Oh, the Darlin boys they all dressed funny.
And the Darlin boys they talked real slow.
But nobody did it like the Darlin boys,
When it came to the old banjo,
When it came to the old banjo.

Albums by the Dillards

Back Porch Bluegrass (Elektra - 1963)
The Dillards Live . . . Almost (Elektra - 1964)
Pickin' and Fiddlin' (Elektra - 1965)
Wheatstraw Suite (Elektra - 1968)
Copperfields (Elektra - 1970)
Roots and Branches (Anthem - 1972)
Tribute to the American Duck (Poppy - 1973)
*The Dillards vs. the Incredible Flying LA Time
     Machine* (Flying Fish - 1977)
Decade Waltz (Flying Fish - 1979)
Mountain Rock (Crystal Clear Records - 1979)
Homecoming and Family Reunion (Flying Fish - 1980)
Let It Fly (Vanguard - 1990)
There Is A Time (Vanguard - 1991)
Take Me Along For The Ride (Vanguard - 1992)

Dillard-Hartford-Dillard

Glitter Grass from the Nashwood Hollyville Strings
     (Flying Fish - 1976)
Permanent Wave (Flying Fish - 1980)

Hey Boys

"We're the Dillards, and we're all from Salem, Missouri, which I'm sure you've all heard of. And we're all hillbillies. I thought I'd better tell you that, 'cause you probably thought we were the Budapest String Quartet."
—Mitch Jayne introducing the Dillards at The Mecca

Comedy proved essential to the Dillards' early success. Mitch Jayne and Rodney Dillard proved as reliable a comic tandem as the Smothers Brothers. In fact, at times the Dillards received too many audience laughs to suit other acts sharing the same stage.

As their star rose in Hollywood, the famed William Morris Agency had signed the Dillards to their stable of talent. Unfortunately, the agency had no idea what to do with the band.

"They had never worked with a bluegrass band before and they really didn't know what to do with us," Dean said. "They sent us out a few times to open for the Smothers Brothers, but that didn't work very well. Our show was a mixture of music and comedy, and the Smothers Brothers didn't like us getting a lot of laughs. We were asked by their staff to tone down the comedy and play more music, as it conflicted with what they were trying to do. But the audiences loved Mitch and his comedy routines. Mitch is a great talker."

The combination of storytelling and slapstick enabled the Dillards to reach audiences who otherwise would have turned a deaf ear to bluegrass.

"A lot of urban people didn't want to have a lot to do with bluegrass, because it was just a bit too close to the house," Rodney said. "When we presented the humor it wasn't the burlesque, baggypants, blacked-out-teeth type of comedy, but rather a more sophisticated variety. To a New Yorker our routine was still corn, but to everyone else it was just plain good, clean comedy. Audiences accepted our humor, image and music as a whole. Ultimately, we were able to transcend a musical barrier. As a result you had this bunch of weirdos from Missouri playing this dinka-dinka banjo stuff in the top clubs in the country for as long as a month at a time."

The Dillards acknowledge David Hammill as playing a key role in the professional development of the Dillards comedy. The group met Hammill at the Buddhi Club while they were stranded in Oklahoma City. Hammill was a one-man show, picking the long-necked banjo, singing folk tunes and performing a "rap"—a comical monologue. Impressed by the Dillards raw talent and enthusiasm, Hammill took it upon himself to take the group under his wing and pass on his own comic knowledge. Late at night when the rest of the Oklahoma City denizens were quietly asleep in their beds, Hammill was schooling Mitch and Rodney on the art of comic timing.

Hammill encouraged the Dillards to draw on their Ozark heritage, to tell more stories on stage and provide the audience with colorful images of Ozark life. Hammill described groups he had seen in other clubs as looking like they had been carved out

"It's possible to observe Rodney," Mitch remarked to audiences grimly, "and understand why some animals eat their young."—*photo courtesy of Douglas Dillard*

of soap. The Dillards, he insisted, offered a fresh approach, as they appeared to have stepped right out of the woods.

Mitch had agreed with Hammill's assessment of bluegrass groups, having viewed dozens before the Dillards had ever left Salem. Constantly confounding Mitch was watching bluegrass groups play "Salty Dog Blues" with the seriousness of a Mozart symphony. So wrapped up in their music were these musicians that the sheer joy and fun of playing bluegrass appeared lost. Audiences left thinking the music was great, but wondering if the players had had a good time. Only a few select groups like Lester Flatt and Earl Scruggs were providing any showmanship during the early 1960s, Mitch remarked.

"Everyone else was playing the straightest, driest, and in the most uninteresting way to put on what was really fun music," Mitch recalled. "At the time I didn't understand the importance of timing. David taught us that while the line has to be funny, timing is still everything."

Hammill suggested that Rodney play the comic foil for Mitch. He explained that Rodney possessed the most expressive face in the group.

"His eyebrows go up to form this little tent," Mitch said. "Nobody has ever looked as stupid as Rodney and still been able to walk and chew gum."

Playing the victim to Mitch's wit never bothered Rodney, as he enjoyed hearing the audience's laughter.

"Mitch is a natural humorist. He's a very funny writer and a funny man. I've got a funny bone and love slapstick humor. When we started the Dillards we sort of naturally fell into the comic routine, with Mitch being the straight man and me being the victim."

Along with Hammill, Mitch credits Howe Teague with teaching him the art of storytelling. The Dillards utilized Teague's fluid storytelling ability to introduce "The Biggest Whatever" on the *Wheatstraw Suite* album. Listeners can hear the sound of Teague rocking on the front porch and trying to describe to tourists the sightings of a big, hairy creature.

Mitch frequently opened the show by lighting his pipe and allowing a big puff of smoke to drift toward the ceiling. He repeated this routine even in clubs which banned smoking. He observed that fans appeared to relax when he lit the pipe, as if they were curled up on a couch watching a fireplace.

A common opener involved the story of the Nash family, which represented the typical Ozark family and helped illustrate the Dillards' heritage. The following is a condensed version of the Nash family's tragic vacation excursion to Yellowstone National Park, as narrated by Mitch Jayne:

"The Nash Family had seventeen children, and I knew all the kids. I always wondered why on earth would somebody want to have seventeen kids? What would be the purpose of it? I found out through the Nashes.

"Now in the Ozarks if you've only got one or two kids, what would you do if they went to the bad and not have meaningful jobs, or marry wrong, or go to jail, or maybe even become a serial killer? But if you've got seventeen children, there is bound to be one or two that will turn out good and come back to support mommy and daddy in their old age. All of the Nashs' seventeen kids grew up and prospered. One of them became a state representative, and one became a TV announcer. One year, the kids decided to pool their money together and send their parents to Yellowstone National Park for a vacation. The kids paid for the whole thing. Bought them a car. Paid for hotel rooms and all their expenses.

"Well, Mr. and Mrs. Nash got out there and promptly got lost. They drove around the park for hours just as lost as geese. Finally they came across a stump in the woods, which had a map on top of it in one of those plexiglass holders. Down in the corner of the map was a red X and the words 'You are here.' Mr. Nash read the message, scratched his head and turned to his wife and

> *said, 'Mamma, how in the heck did they know that?'*
> *This was a perfect introducer to the Dillards. This told*
> *the audience that these are the type of people that we*
> *(the Dillards) come from. We were as lost as geese too."*

The Dillards discovered quickly that audiences relished references to moonshine. Two songs, "Ebo Walker" and "Dooley," were originally simple tunes about producers and consumers of corn liquor, but they gradually grew into large segments of the Dillards' act.

Simple stories used to introduce songs often evolved into long narratives, with each band member spontaneously throwing in one-liners on stage. "Ebo Walker" is a prime example of a modest story woven into an outlandish tale. Sadly, Ebo Walker died tragically, but at least his death provided the Dillards with one final story. The following is Mitch's account of the lamentable demise of Ebo Walker, with help from Rodney and Dean.

> *"We had an ole boy back home named Ebo Walker, and*
> *me and Rodney made up a song about him. There are*
> *guys like Ebo in every small town. Ebo was the kind of*
> *guy that trying to get him to actually do a day's work is*
> *like trying to nail jelly to the wall. Now Ebo was bad to*
> *drink. Not just moonshine, mind you, but he drank*
> *things like tractor radiator alcohol, Liquid Wrench, and*
> *the like. One morning Ebo went out on the back porch to*
> *check the thermometer and it was bitter cold. Well, that*
> *Liquid Wrench works fast, and pretty soon he decided he*
> *better make a trip to the privy. While he was out there,*
> *he put in and died.*
> *   "Ebo wasn't much of a noticeable kind of guy. 'Bout*
> *his third day missing, his old lady got to feeling a bit*
> *uneasy about him, so she sent one of the little bufords*
> *out to find out what had happened to daddy. The little*

*buford returned and in true Ozark fashion he told his
mommy just like it was, that daddy 'was out there froze
up stiffer than a woodpecker's lip' in the privy.*

*"Well, it was cold weather and he had set up real
good, no play on words there. They didn't have a hearse,
but he was so stiff they wondered just how they were
going to load him up into the family car. They just set
him up in the front seat like anybody else. At the time of
his death, Ebo had been reaching for some toilet paper
and it froze that way, so they stuck his hand out the
window and everybody they passed thought he was just
waving.*

*"Now, Ebo, like we said before, was bad to drink. He
had drank so much moonshine in his life that when they
buried him it just seeped into the ground. He killed
every bit of grass fifty feet 'round his grave, and
promptly resurrected two Jehovah's Witnesses."*

Mitch once wrote a television treatment for a situation comedy tentatively titled *Another Day, Another
Dillard.* The concept involved the Dillards' experiences in a poor rural community. Dean was to play a
crazed inventor, and Rodney a mental pygmy who
tried to blow out light bulbs. Douglas' character just
sat around all day and played the banjo. To illustrate
the town's poverty, one of the jokes was that the
dimes had been passed around so much that they
had become incredibly thin. When someone dropped
a dime, it didn't fall to the floor—it fluttered to the
ground like a feather. Unfortunately, the idea was
never picked up by a network.

When the Dillards reunited for a tour in 1989,
Mitch carted his treasure chest of homespun stories
out from the closet, dusted his favorite gems off and
dressed them up for the stage.

Touring in Japan posed a slight dilemma for

Mitch. True, English was a common second language among Japanese citizens—but Mitch didn't speak normal English. Mitch spoke the Ozark version. Mitch questioned whether he should even attempt to tell the stories, but the group's Japanese guide encouraged him to stick with the routine.

On stage one night, Mitch found himself bored with the "Old Blue" gag, and decided to spice things up a bit. Staring into a sea of intense faces, Mitch strayed completely from the traditional "Old Blue" script. The joke came to him while on stage:

A family decided one year to surprise their mom by digging a new privy, Mitch said. Unfortunately, the boys forgot to tell her, and one night when she felt the urge to go outside, she wandered out in the dark and fell into the latrine hole, covering herself in not so nice things. Desperate for help, the woman screamed "Fire!" The boys ran out and rescued their unfortunate mother.

Curious about her choice of words, one of the boys asked why she yelled fire. "Well," retorted the woman, "Had I yelled #@!*, you wouldn't have come." The story left Dean, Rodney and Douglas paralyzed by laughter. Meanwhile, the Japanese audience was gawking at Mitch in stunned silence, looking extremely panicky like a deer caught in the headlights.

The response alarmed Mitch initially, but he then suddenly realized the reason for the anxious murmurs emanating from the theater.

"What they had done was very typical of the Japanese," Mitch said. "They had memorized *The Dillards Live . . . Almost*. They knew the song, and the story I was supposed to use to introduce the song.

Mitch has always
had a talent for
weaving a magical
spell over any
audience.
—*photo courtesy of
Mitch Jayne*

But I had left my script and had told a completely
different story than the one they had memorized
phonetically, and I had lost them."

"Dooley" was another audience favorite and represented a compilation of moonshiners Mitch and the
rest of the Dillards had met while living in the
Ozarks. Mitch had even helped a friend run a batch
of moonshine once, just to learn how it was done. He
learned that brewing corn liquor was more work

than he had bargained for, and that he'd rather just stay on the consumer end of the operation.

The story involving Dooley varied through the years. The following offers a brief taste of what audiences learned to savor while listening to Mitch concoct his own brew of stories.

> *"We wrote this song about an old man back home that made moonshine whiskey for about twenty-five years. Drinking moonshine whiskey is perfectly all right, if you want to get so drunk that you have to hang on to the grass to lean against the ground. Wake up in the morning with snail tracks all over your clothes. Well, we we changed this man's name to Dooley, but the song is true. Now, making moonshine wasn't any great wonder, as a lot of people did that. But this old man never got caught, never went to jail, and never was arrested. And it wasn't because they didn't know that he was making moonshine. On Saturdays he'd back his truck up to the only store in town and load five hundred-pound sacks of sugar into the back of the truck. I don't know how much you know about making moonshine, but they knew he wasn't making fudge up there. Well, this old man had two daughters. I used to be a school teacher and I taught one of them. These were what we called big mammoth girls back home. These were the type of girls, well, there is an old Ozark saying that if you lifted up one arm, two bats and a whippoorwill would fly out."*

Mitch kept audiences amused with explanations of the Ozark accent and expressions such as "pillow" instead of "pillar" and "pillar" instead of "pillow." Common misuses of words tickled Mitch and his audiences, at times to the point of tears.

An Ozark citizen for instance, puts "tire" on the roof and "tars" on his car. Ozarkians own "Cockerel Spaniard" dogs and raise "black Anguish" cattle, and are occasionally employed as state highway "petroleum."

"Some of these people misused half the English language in the nicest kind of ways," Mitch declared. "Those words come at you and they are so near to right, like the first time I heard a man say 'bullnozer.' He said, 'I'm going to have a bullnozer dig out my pond.' The word sounds like that it's exactly what he means—a bull is going to root up his pond. I've always liked 'back-hole digger,' because that is what it does. It digs up holes and the bucket is in the back."

The following excerpts from Mitch's various commentaries provide a sampling of everyday misuses of the English language.

"A lady who was more into description than medical accuracy told me once that her husband had had a 'cerbal hermage of the heart' and they had to put him on 'auction.' You didn't know whether to send him a get well card or bid on him.

"An old man had an antique store, and he had a little old marble top table that he was trying to sell me. He slammed his fist on that table as hard as he could and pronounced, 'This thing is as solid as the Rock of Gabriel.' It sounded right to him. He'd probably never seen Gibraltar, but he had probably read about Gabriel in the Bible.

"There was this guy who cut wood for me and he had a great big strapping son, like most of these kids who grew up in the woods and worked in the sawmills. He was just as strong as the day is long. He had taken up turkey hunting, and one morning when he brought my wood he said, 'Mike, this is amazing. I shot a gobbler just before I got to the turn of your approach and I blowed his head off. I went to pick it up and it was gone. That ought to be in the World's Book Of Genius.' But

his dad said, 'Son, you've got that wrong. That's the World's Book Of Genesis.'

"Another friend of mine described his brother as 'sober as a jug when he run over that service station pump!'

"Making things short and to the point is important to hill people, as with my friend who told me about his wife's pacemaker. 'Heck, the woman's run by electric,' he told me in wonder, 'She takes bat'ries.'"

Drawing on his years as a teacher, Mitch also entertained listeners with stories about his favorite pupils.

"Stanley Crocker was a great student but plain could not learn numbers. I worked with him and worked with him and tried everything I knew to teach him his numbers, but nothing worked. He didn't have any problem with anything else, like remembering the names of all the states, but he had some kind of mental block when it came to counting.

"Well, I couldn't graduate him from the first grade until he learned to count to ten. It was one of things required, along with knowing how to write your name. So, I'd get him up there every day and have his back to the class so he wouldn't get embarrassed, and start working on him. I'd rare back and say, 'How many is this?' I'd hold up a finger and he'd say, 'One.' Then I'd hold up another finger and say, 'Now how many is this?' And he'd say, 'Two.' He might have a little trouble on three and maybe bog down completely on four.

"It was getting awful near pressing time for him to graduate, and I had gotten him up to eight the day before. So, I told him, 'Stanley, today we are going to do it. We are going to make it to ten.' It came time to recite Stanley, so I got him up there and sat him in front of my desk. I wanted to make him all comfortable. He sat there with his little hands clasped on the front of the desk. I rared back and put my feet on the desk so we could both be totally comfortable. I said, 'Now Stanley,

yesterday we quit on eight and today it's over the top. How much is this?' And I held up eight fingers.

"The little fella just sat there and his little face just turned into a knot like a prune. I didn't know what had happened to the child. All I knew was that he had broken down and had these huge tears running down his face. I said, 'Stanley, it's just numbers, don't get mad at me. I'm going to have to teach you for another nine years or ten, but it's okay. It's just that you were doing so well yesterday, and I had my hopes up so big for you.' About that time Stanley's sister came up to use the pencil sharpener and said, 'Mr. Jayne, you've got Stanley's fingers caught inside the desk drawer.'

"I had mashed his fingers right across the knuckles, and he wasn't going to say anything. I felt so bad I went ahead and passed him anyway."

The Whole World 'Round

"Fiddle and the bow and the firelight's glow, you can hear that lonesome sound. I'll leave behind my troublin' mind and go the whole world 'round"
— Chorus of "The Whole World 'Round"

The group's dream of seeing the world began when they left Salem and has yet to end, although there have been a few narrow misses. Once, during a tour with the Ventures, the two bands gave thirty-one concerts in thirty days. They drove to each destination, with all of the stops seemingly at least five hundred miles apart. Traveling through the Rocky Mountains, the boys ran into a blizzard but pressed forward, down an ice-covered highway without the security of snow tires or chains. Douglas was navigating the group's station wagon down treacherously frozen slopes while the rest of the band members slept, not realizing the danger which surrounded them.

"There was a ten-thousand-foot drop on either side, and the road was a solid sheet of ice. I was scared to death, while everybody else was sleeping like babies," Douglas said.

Dean recalled returning from a concert in Boulder, Colorado when a disaster occurred in Utah. A car had spun out on the freeway and had come to a stop in the center of the road. Dean had just finished driving a double shift, and was trying to grab a moment's rest stretched out on the back seat. His sleep was interrupted when Irv Duggan, the Dillards' road manager and sometime bass player, reached across the back seat and jostled him back to consciousness.

"He said, 'Hang on tight, we're going over!' When you wake up and that is the first thing you hear, you're thinking, 'What are we going over?' Fortunately, nobody got hurt. The equipment was packed so tight in the van nothing got damaged, although the van got totaled out," Dean said.

Rodney once flipped the band's van off a twenty-foot embankment and landed in a creek bed while returning home from a gig in Montana. After successfully maneuvering through all the mountain passes (which had been closed by the state highway patrol), Rodney thought he was home free. He was listening to a Tammy Wynette tape, hoping it would keep him awake because her voice irritated him. Unfortunately, it put him to sleep on the ice. Again, the band members escaped any serious injury.

On tour with the Byrds, the bands flew from concert to concert on a chartered DC-3. Douglas remembers looking out the cabin window in horror as he spotted another aircraft bearing down on the Dillards' plane. Bone-chilling seconds elapsed as the Dillards' pilot miraculously maneuvered the craft out of the path of the charging airplane and narrowly avoided a mid-air collision which would have brought a premature end to both the Byrds and the Dillards.

Later during the same junket, the bands were fly-

The Dillards eventually traded in their buckskins for cooler gear.
(l-r) Douglas, Dean, Rodney & Mitch.   —*photo courtesy of the Dillards*

ing across the Rocky Mountains when their plane hit
an air pocket and instantly dropped a thousand feet.
Both Rodney and Douglas passed out, believing that
this was the end.

Jim Dickson had arranged for the Byrds and the
Dillards to travel cross country together on a thirty-
stop tour. Both bands recorded at World Pacific Studio and were friends; Dean had actually assisted the
Byrds in developing their first hit record. Driving
home late one night, Dean happened to pass by
World Pacific and noticed Jim Dickson's Volkswagen
parked on the lot. Lights shone from the building,
raising Dean's curiosity. Inside, Dickson was vainly
attempting to settle a loud argument involving members of the Byrds. The folk-rock group were divided
on how the harmony should sound on a particular
song they were attempting to record. Dean was
drawn into the dispute and asked to solve the dilemma.

"I told Jim (Dickson) to get those other two guys
out of the studio, then I took (Roger) McGuinn in
and we sang together. McGuinn sang lead and I sang
tenor. When that was done, I sang the baritone part."

The Byrds carefully followed Dean's musical direction, and easily recorded the song in straight triad
harmony. The result was the Byrds' first commercial
hit record, "Mr. Tambourine Man."

The Byrds/Dillards tour itself was somewhat unusual, as it mixed four hillbillies with four rock-and-
rollers. The tour included stopovers in numerous
small college towns. Often the students, who came
from farming communities, could relate better to the
Dillards than to the Byrds.

"Whoever booked that tour must've been on blotter acid or something," Mitch chuckled. "We were playing in towns, like some place in Minnesota, which were only large enough to have a crowd. We would sell the concerts out, and the crowds could understand what the Dillards were doing. They weren't bluegrass people, but they were used to the country element of music, and the instruments we played were familiar to them. If we had had an accordion, we'd have fit right in."

The Byrds, on the other hand, were an esoteric band playing Bob Dylan songs. Rural American teenagers weren't sure what to think of the Byrds, although they were aware that the Byrds were supposed to be rock stars.

At the time of the tour, various members of the Byrds were into drugs, mushrooms, visions, and dream interpretation. They decorated the windows of the DC-3 with pieces of colored cellophane, giving it a stained-glass appearance.

"It was the weirdest airplane to look into or out of that I've ever seen. I was never sure if we were going to get that plane off the ground," Mitch said.

Early into the tour Rodney had a nightmare about a horrible plane crash. He then made the mistake of sharing his dream with the Byrds. Panic set in as word of Rodney's dream buzzed through the cabin. Louisville was scheduled as the final leg of the journey. As the tour grew closer to an end the anxiety level increased, until finally the day came for the flight to Louisville.

"Some members of the Byrds refused to fly on the plane to Louisville," Dean recalled. "It was a tense flight, but it went without a hitch and we landed safely."

Mitch was intrigued by other aspects of the Byrds tour. Each time the groups performed, the Byrds' road manager collected half of the concert receipts. Half of the money went to the Byrds, and half to the Dillards. Never before had Mitch seen money accumulate so quickly. Never before had Mitch seen money disappear so easily and so frequently. The problem was that money didn't seem to have any particular value to the road manager, nor did he have any concept of the receipts' importance to the Dillards.

"He stored the money in an old cardboard suitcase that was already coming apart and had dime store hinges. I was fascinated by this, because I'd never seen so much money in my life. When we got to Chicago late in the tour he had well over one hundred thousand dollars in that suitcase," Mitch said. "All through the tour I had watched it grow, in increments of fifteen thousand, thirty thousand and forty thousand. The thing was just bulging with money, and literally had bills sticking out of the cracks. He eventually had to get someone to sit on it in order to close the thing."

What disconcerted Mitch the most was not the ragged state of the suitcase, but its location. At times no one knew just where it was, as it frequently got left behind. During the tour the suitcase was left in taxicabs twice, on buses, at airports, and abandoned in hotel lobbies. Once, Mitch spotted the Dillards' hard-earned cash sitting on a hotel loading dock.

Shortly after checking into the groups' hotel in Chicago, Mitch paid a visit to the Byrds' road manager. Once inside, the manager nonchalantly inquired if Mitch had noticed the suitcase lying around anywhere recently. Alarmed by the question, Mitch exclaimed that he hadn't seen it since the previous stop. The manager calmly told Mitch not to worry, adding that he was certain the suitcase was bound to pop up eventually.

"I told him, 'Hey, your mind is off in gopher land or something. We'd better start hunting down that suitcase now!'" Mitch said remembering that nerve-wracking search for the band's cash.

Mitch hustled downstairs to the lobby and frantically began a systematic search of the hotel. His eyes finally locked onto an old porter who was casually seated on top of the suitcase.

"I knew the suitcase had more than a hundred thousand dollars inside it. I went over to the porter and said as calmly as possible, 'That suitcase belongs to us.' The porter looked at me and said, 'Is this your suitcase? We didn't know whose it was, so I put it back on the cab and had them take it to the airport. Nobody at the airport claimed it, so they brung it back here.' It had been sitting there for more than an hour," Mitch said, still shaking his head in disbelief more than twenty years later.

Later during the same tour, Mitch visited the road manager again. This time, Mitch immediately realized that at least the money wasn't missing. The road manager was standing naked as a jaybird and counting a fistful of bills. He cursed at Mitch and told him that the interruption had made him lose count.

"The entire bed and floor was covered in pillow-size piles of money. He had bills in his hand, hundred dollar bills stuck to the bottom of each foot,'

Mitch laughed shaking his head as he relived that bizarre encounter.

Given the comic nature of the journey, Mitch felt obligated to maintain a journal of his adventures. The result was a two-hundred-page manuscript, *Eight More Miles to Louisville*, but before he could sell the work the manuscript was lost.

"Losing the manuscript was a real shame, because it was one of the funniest things I've ever written," Mitch said.

Douglas' strangest journey, however, came later in his career, with the Doug Dillard Expedition. On a Trans World Airlines flight bound for Hawaii a fellow passenger went berserk, threatened to kill everyone on board, and set Douglas' hair on fire with a cigarette lighter. Douglas escaped serious injury, and the attacker was finally subdued.

Retrospectively, Mitch argued that Douglas and strange events always seemed to go hand in hand.

"One time Douglas and a group of friends were leaving a yacht that had been leased by Harry Nilsson for a party. As they headed to shore, Jimmy Webb dropped a contact lens into the surf. Douglas reached down and picked it up. If this story had been told about anyone else, I wouldn't have believed it, but those type of things were always happening to Douglas. He was always picking a contact lens out of the surf," Mitch declared.

Unusual stage partners were common occurrences early in the group's career, as the Dillards followed every imaginable act from motorcycle-riding chimpanzees to acrobatic elephants. While audiences were always guaranteed a solid performance by the Dil-

On the set of *The Judy Garland Show*. Judy spent so much on the boys' tuxedoes that there wasn't any money left in the budget for socks or shoes.   —*photo courtesy of Douglas Dillard*

lards, they never knew how the other acts on the bill would pan out. "During one show, one of the daredevil motorcycle chimps lost control of his bike and drove off stage into the orchestra pit," Douglas said with a laugh.

Not all of the performers who opened for the Dillards belonged in a zoo. Occasionally, the band shared billing with an unknown comic who would later become a major Hollywood box office draw— Steve Martin. Long after he attained success, Martin, a banjo player himself, performed "Doug's Tune" on *The Tonight Show*. Early in the band's career, Bill Cosby opened for the group. Later on, the roles were reversed and the Dillards opened for Cosby.

Motorcycle-maniac chimps weren't the only ones with vehicle problems. During their heyday, the Dillards traveled in a Chevrolet Corvair van. The van was always breaking down, and causing more headaches for the band than it was worth. One night the Dillards were scheduled to perform at the Golden Bear Club in Huntington Beach, California. Instead of riding with his friends in the van, Douglas decided to drive out later in his own car.

"I was driving along the (Pacific) Coast Highway when I saw the familiar Corvair van sitting on the side of the highway engulfed in flames. Rodney, Dean and Mitch were all holding hands, singing and dancing around the van like it was some campfire," Douglas said.

The Dillards were dancing with glee, Mitch explained, because they were hoping the fire meant the end of the dreaded Corvair van. Their joy later transformed into bitter sorrow when the repair shop informed the insurance company that the van could still be salvaged.

Multiple television appearances on other shows came their way after *The Andy Griffith Show*, but none proved as successful as the Darlings. Among the Dillards' credits include appearances on *The Joey Bishop Show* and *Playboy After Dark*. They were also signed for seven episodes of the ill-fated and poorly-conceived *The Judy Garland Show*.

While on the road in Pennsylvania, the group received an urgent wire from a William Morris Agency representative. The agency was summoning the Dillards back to California immediately in order to appear on *The Judy Garland Show*. The agency had signed the group for a seven-week engagement on the variety show. Excited by the prospect of performing with a living legend, the Dillards rushed back to Los Angeles only to find disappointment waiting on the other side of the rainbow.

They arrived at the studio expecting to meet the singer who had captured audiences' hearts as Dorothy in the *The Wizard of Oz*. Instead, they met an actress who appeared tired and sad. She looked terribly fragile, and her voice would only last for about three songs before giving out. When the famed actress shook hands with the Dillards, they were shocked to see her scarred wrists, reminders of previous suicide attempts.

Nothing on the set was similar to the camaraderie and closeness of *The Andy Griffith Show* experience. Appearing on *The Judy Garland Show* was as if the fates wanted to demonstrate to the Dillards just what the polar opposite of *The Andy Griffith Show* was all about.

"The star of the show sets the tone for everyone else on the set. Andy's attitude was one of good humor and patience. If Andy never lost his patience, then why should anyone else?" Mitch reasoned.

Crew members on the Garland set scurried around like dazed ants, unsure of the show's direction. The problem was that the directions received by the writers, musicians, sound crew and lighting crew were all subject to change at the drop of a hat. No one knew whether Garland would actually sing the scheduled songs or whether she would back off and sing something totally different. Mel Torme, the show's music director, appeared to the Dillards to be a nervous wreck. In the end, the Dillards performed with Garland dressed in tuxedos and barefoot.

"We did one *Judy Garland Show,* and were paid for the second show even though we didn't perform," Dean recalled. "I think that was to buy out our contract. The problem with *The Judy Garland Show* was that the direction of the show changed from week to week."

A similar miscasting occurred when the Dillards were signed to perform on Hugh Hefner's *Playboy After Dark.* When the Dillards arrived, they found a set full of men wearing smoking jackets and actresses dressed up as sex kittens. The set left the boys feeling as if they had stepped into some bachelor's den of iniquity. The only line the Dillards had on the show came when Hefner introduced the band to Barbie Benton.

"We were supposed to look at her and say, 'Hi, Barbie.' Well, there is no way you can say 'Hi, Barbie,' straight. Rodney said later that we all sounded like a bunch of ducks," Mitch laughed.

The band was also frequently seen on music-oriented programs such as *Where The Action Is, Hollywood-A-Go-Go, Hootenanny* and *Shindig.* Formats for these television shows often resulted in odd visual mixtures. For instance, while the band played traditional bluegrass songs on *Hollywood-A-Go-Go,* they were backed up by wildly clad, leggy girls dancing frantically behind the Dillards in white go-go boots. Sharing the stage with the Dillards on other occa-

Bluegrass and Go Go Girls collided on *Hollywood-A-Go-Go*.
Note that Mitch is playing an electric bass.
—*photo courtesy of Dean Webb*

sions were bands such Paul Revere and the Raiders
and Buffalo Springfield, which featured Stephen
Stills.

Infrequent appearances on television shows like
The Andy Griffith Show didn't guarantee guest stars
instant stardom or name recognition. Hillbilly
clothing and makeup also didn't help the Dillards
become easily recognizable to casual observers, as
proven once in Phoenix, Arizona.

"We were traveling through Arizona one afternoon, and a police officer stopped our van right outside of Phoenix while I was driving. Apparently, I fit
the description of a guy who had just robbed a bank.
We explained that we were musicians, and they let

us go once they verified our identity," Douglas remembered.

Brushes with the law are comical in retrospect,
but when the incidents occurred, the Dillards puz-
zled over why their faces frightened law enforcement
officials so frequently. Once while appearing at The
Cellar Door in Georgetown, Dean and Mitch were ac-
costed by the local constabulary. Rodney was looking
out the window of his hotel room when he saw police officers throw his fellow band members up
against the wall. It was a case of mistaken identity,
but it was neither the first nor the last.

"Once, after Mitch had left the group, Dean and I
were bringing the van back from a show in Utah and
were stopped by the highway patrol," Rodney said.
"There were no windows in the rear of the van, so
we thought we were just being stopped for speeding.
The officer calmly asked us to get out of the van, so
we came out the side doors to find about fifteen state
troopers and FBI agents pointing guns at us. Someone driving a blue van similar to our had robbed a
service station and killed two people. One of the sus-
pects apparently had a mustache, which Dean had at
the time."

Early in the Dillards' career they accepted a book-
ing in Sioux Falls, South Dakota. On the surface the
gig sounded pretty inviting—three days for five
thousand dollars. In order to reach the club on time,
the Dillards flew at their own expense to South Dakota, checked into a motel and grabbed a taxi.

Instead of a quiet club such as The Troubadour or
The Mecca, the taxi pulled up to a long building. At
first glance, the Dillards realized William Morris had
booked them into a plain roadhouse.

"It was a long building like you would expect to raise turkeys in. They had put booths lining both sides of the building and a little stage in the middle of this place. We were going to be performing for a bunch of half-drunk, good ole boys and probably get ourselves caught up in the biggest fight of our lives. The only thing that was missing was the chicken wire," Mitch laughed.

What appeared next was the clincher. As their eyes adjusted to the dimly lit, smoke-filled room, two musicians dressed in sequined outfits started a number to introduce the next act—a stripper. The Dillards promptly turned around, left, and drove back to the motel. They booked the next flight back to Los Angeles and chalked the episode up to experience.

A similar mishap occurred in Las Vegas when the Dillards, dressed in their traditional buckskin costumes, found themselves booked into a lounge for a week-long run. The entire audience consisted of five large drunks. Before the band finished their opening number, the curtain suddenly closed in front of the stage. Stunned and angry, the Dillards demanded to know why the curtain had been pulled. The casino pit boss approached Rodney and explained the situation.

"He told us that they were trying to upgrade the club's image and suggested that we wear nice suits instead of buckskins," Rodney remembered.

Instead of complying, the Dillards stormed off stage. Angered by their refusal to change wardrobe and musical style, the pit boss yelled that they would never play in Vegas again. Driving back to the hotel, Rodney repeatedly stole furtive glances out the back window of the van, fearful of retribution.

"Rodney had this idea that the place we were playing was probably mob operated. He half expected guys with tommy guns to be coming after us," Mitch joked.

Perhaps the band's most disastrous engagement occurred on New Year's Eve at The Cellar Door. The Dillards always lived by the rule that they would never perform on New Year's Eve. Temptation got the best of the group, unfortunately, when the management of The Cellar Door offered the band a considerable sum for a single night's performance. Against their better judgement, the Dillards snatched the offer and prepared for the nightmare to come— which is exactly what occurred.

The trouble with New Year's Eve parties is that they are parties. Clubgoers on New Year's Eve are destined to wear silly hats (sometimes costumes), carry an assortment of noise-makers, yell loudly at anyone who will listen, and feel almost morally obligated to get drunk. This dynamic mixture was not the normal Dillard crowd.

"This is the worst possible crowd for a group whose act is gentle humor and fun music. You had guys trying to pick up some loose chick, and everybody else is mad because they weren't invited to a better party. It was awful. We had drunks rolling around arguing, and people getting into fights with their wives. Rodney couldn't get the music to work, and the comedy sure wasn't working," Mitch said.

Frustrated and irritable, the band left the stage after the first set and retreated to the sanctuary of the club's roof. They wanted to escape the madness below, watch the fireworks, and blow off a little steam. An argument erupted as to why in heaven's name they had accepted the job, and it nearly came to blows between Rodney and Mitch. Calm was restored without violence, and the group trudged down for the last show. Afterward, the group gathered in the dressing room and solemnly swore that they would never again play on New Year's Eve.

Rodney preferred to play in the smaller listening-room clubs, such as the Pasadena Ice House or The Cellar Door. They provided the ideal atmosphere for the Dillards' brand of entertainment.

"These weren't bars, but rather small mini-theaters or listening rooms. I had trouble playing in huge theaters, because the energy just seemed to disperse. When we toured with Elton John on the Honky Chateau Tour in 1972 all we played was large houses, but we were electrified," he said.

The British rocker had caught the Dillards' act one night in Los Angeles at The Troubadour. He had been searching for a band which would represent the roots of American music in order to better complement his own performance, and the Dillards fit the bill. He contacted the group a short time later and signed them to a thirty-day cross-country tour, his first in America.

"Elton was a lot of fun to work with," Dean said. "He worked incredibly hard and would do these Jerry Lee Lewis-type of moves even during warm-ups."

Crowds on the Elton John tour received the Dillards warmly, Mitch added, because the Dillards were a dramatic departure from what they expected.

"These were rock and roll fans, not bluegrass fans. Most of them didn't know us, but since we were with Elton John they figured we must be hot stuff," Mitch reasoned.

Not coincidentally, the Dillards' album *Roots and Branches*, released during the time of the Elton John tour, became the Dillards' most commercially successful album to that point. The album hit the forties on the *Billboard* and *Cashbox* charts. While Rodney favored playing for smaller audiences, the Dillards never missed a chance to play at huge festivals. Through the years they appeared at the Monterey Pop Festival and the Newport Folk Festival, where Rodney allegedly threw up on Bob Dylan, a charge leveled by fellow Dillards' members and one which he steadfastly denies.

Playing these special events allowed the Dillards to share the stage with performers destined to become legends in the music industry, such as Dylan, Pete Seeger, Arlo Guthrie, Peter, Paul and Mary, and countless other recording stars. Outdoor concerts in expansive settings created technical difficulties for the Dillards. Mitch recalled the breathtaking enormity of looking out into the audience section of the Hollywood Bowl for the first time. The Dillards were scheduled to perform with Joan Baez and Judy Collins and had gone to the Bowl early to perform a soundcheck. Gazing into the audience seating Rodney and Mitch realized immediately that they would have to live or die by the quality of the music.

"It was the biggest place we had ever played. Rodney and I looked out into this vast sea of empty seats and he turned to me and said, 'We're going to have to play this like Shakespearean actors.' I knew what he meant. We were going to have to use big gestures and big takes, because to the people in the back would have to have binoculars to tell who we were. There were maybe a hundred rows that could

The Dillards let their music do the talking at the Hollywood
Bowl.   —*photo courtesy of* Bluegrass Unlimited

see us, but that was a long way off. We knew we
would live or die by the music, because the comedy
was not going to work. So we decided that along
with the music, I would just tell some stories," Mitch
explained.

A series of life changes forced Mitch to make a
career decision in 1974. He had recently divorced
Lee, and his two daughters had graduated from high
school. His desire to devote himself to full-time writing was intensified by the sale of the movie rights of
Old Fish Hawk to 20th Century Fox. More disturbing
to Mitch was that he was losing his hearing. He suddenly found himself in the unnerving position of being unable to note true on the bass and occasionally
singing either flat or sharp.

"There were only four instruments in our group.

It's not like playing an orchestra where you might get lost if you hit a clam. Any mistakes you made, if you sang the least bit flat or sharp, were easily heard, and that bothered me. I had this money from *Fish Hawk* and I thought 'this is the last time that I'll have this much money all at once to use as a grubstake,'" he said.

Like the narrator in *Hey Boys*, Mitch had gone to the city, gotten a little older, and learned the good sense to return to the Ozarks. He had come to the conclusion that he had enjoyed just as much as he could stand of California, and the yearning for Missouri grew with each passing day. Leaving the Dillards saddened Mitch, but he knew that it was the right decision, and that the band would continue to be successful even without him, as it had when Douglas left six years earlier.

"Wherever Rodney Dillard was, that is where the Dillards were. He was always the leader. He was always the one who directed the music, and where the band was going. As long as Rodney was there, I knew the band was going to survive and do all right," Mitch said.

There Is
A Time

*"So do your roaming in the spring-time, and find
your love in the summer sun. The frost will come
and bring the harvest, and you can sleep when
the day is done."*
                                            —Mitch Jayne

Douglas Dillard

Immediately upon his departure from the Dillards,
Douglas accepted an offer from the Byrds and em-
barked on a world tour. The tour afforded him the
opportunity to visit England, where he met Mick
Jagger. The Rolling Stones' lead singer sneaked Douglas into Stonehenge in order to witness a breathtaking sunrise, but they were snared by efficient consta-
bles. A few kind words by Jagger to the bobbies
relieved the momentary tension, and the party was
able to retreat quietly the same way it had entered.

Returning to the States, Douglas recorded his first
solo album, aptly entitled *The Banjo Album* (recently
re-released on compact disc by Sierra). His sudden
availability resulted in his appearing as a guest performer on albums recorded by such performers as
the Beach Boys, Hoyt Axton, Kay Starr, and Arlo
Guthrie. He built a reputation as a solid sessions mu-

sician and appeared in a diverse collection of recordings, from "What Am I Doing Hanging Round with the Monkees" to the Grammy-Award-winning single "Gentle On My Mind" with Glen Campbell. "Gentle On My Mind" was composed by John Hartford, the Dillards' longtime friend.

Douglas found time to take a short departure from the banjo and play the fiddle for Linda Ronstadt in her recording of "I'll Be Your Baby Tonight."

Television appearances also kept Douglas occupied, as he wrote songs for performed in *Dean Martin's Country Music USA* summer replacement show. He also wrote and performed scores for 7-Up, Kentucky Fried Chicken, Chevrolet, and Visa commercials.

"Douglas is probably, of all the banjo players I've met and known, the most absolutely unique banjo player. Listening to commercials or albums you could always pick out Douglas playing. It is amazing to me that his style is so distinguishable, but I could always tell the feel and flavor that he put into his music," Mitch noted.

When creative differences convinced the late Gene Clark to leave the Byrds, Clark and Douglas teamed up to form the Dillard and Clark Expedition. The group also included Bernie Leadon, who went on to help create the original Eagles. Clark and Douglas collaborated for three years and recorded two albums, *The Fantastic Expedition of Dillard and Clark* in 1968 and *Through the Morning, Through the Night* in 1969. The *Rolling Stone Record Guide* praised the debut album, noting that it "*successfully combines Dillard's iconoclastic bluegrass sensibilities with Clark's*

Douglas Dillard is shown here with the original Kentucky Colonel himself, Harlan Sanders.
—*photo courtesy of Douglas Dillard*

wonderfully warm singing. The Dillard-Clark albums rank with the Byrds' 'Sweetheart of the Rodeo' and the Flying Burrito Brothers' records as country-rock pioneers that still sound better than almost anything that's followed."

Despite their artistic differences, Douglas and Rodney continued to work together on individual projects. The two brothers and Byron Berline were reunited in 1979 on the feature film *The Rose*, which starred Bette Midler. The trio played musicians in Harry Dean Stanton's band, and their faces could be seen on the screen for around ten minutes.

Douglas' second feature film appearance came a year later in Robert Altman's *Popeye*, which starred Robin Williams. The movie was shot in Malta, and when the production lights and cameras shut down for the day, the real adventures started.

"Robin Williams is the most incredible individual I've ever had the fortune to meet. At night we would run up and down the island, which is roughly nineteen miles long, and hit all the clubs. He would get up on stage and play his harmonica while I would play the banjo. He had this uncanny ability to make up lyrics to songs right on the spot while I played as fast as I could. I still don't believe that guy," Douglas said shaking his head as he laughed.

One of Douglas' more unusal film performances came as a result of a walk along Hollywood Boulevard. Douglas happened to bump into a friend of his girlfriend. The mutual acquaintance told Douglas that 20th Century Fox was in need of a four-minute instrumental for use in a chase scene in the movie *Vanishing Point*. The catch was that they needed the song in less than twenty-four hours. No problem! Douglas hurried home and contacted Byron Berline. The pair burned the midnight oil creating the song, "Runaway Country." The next morning they played it for the film's producers, and it was eagerly received.

"We actually recorded the song in the studio while we watched this little moviola of the scene," Douglas explained.

Jack Hoffman and Douglas Dillard collaborated together to produce a textbook, *The Bluegrass Banjo Style of Douglas Flint Dillard*, published in 1980 by Almo Publications. The book includes the fundamental instructions for bluegrass banjo pickers, left hand techniques, and the sheet music for many of the Dillards' most popular tunes.

A tremendous thrill for the banjo picker came during the 1989 Dillards Reunion Tour. During a stop in Japan, Douglas was approached by a throng of starry-eyed teen-age Japanese girls. They weren't groupies, but bluegrass musicians and hard core fans of the Dillards. Upon cornering him, the group broke into a rousing rendition of "Doug's Tune."

"Bluegrass music continues to grow in popularity throughout the world. They have bluegrass bands in Russia, Czechoslovakia, Japan and England. It is a universal type of music, and to hear it being played in other countries really gives me a thrill," he asserted.

The banjo picker remains the true road hog of the original Dillards. While the rest of his compatriots have adopted a more sedentary lifestyle, Douglas is happiest when he is on the road, performing before audiences large and small. The Doug Dillard Band travels north to Alaska annually for a three-week engagement, and are regular performers at "Mayberry Days," held each year at Andy Griffith's home town of Mount Airy, North Carolina.

Douglas continues to record albums with his Doug Dillard Band. The group's 1989 album *Heartbreak Hotel*, produced by brother Rodney, garnered a Grammy nomination in the bluegrass category. Douglas was later honored in February 1994, when he was inducted into the Bluegrass Hall of Greats at the Roy Acuff Theater in Nashville. Although his band has included several musicians, the current Doug Dillard Band consists of lead singer Ginger Boatwright (a member for fourteen years), guitarist Roger Rasnake, mandolinist Jim Langford, and bass player Donnie Clark.

Reflecting on his career, Douglas relates his time with the Dillards as the most satisfying period of his

Douglas Dillard, Mae Axton and Ginger Boatwright celebrate the 1989 Grammy nomination for *Heartbreak Hotel*.
—*photo courtesy of Douglas Dillard*

musical life. Not surprisingly, Douglas' favorite Dillards albums are those he was a part of: *Back Porch Bluegrass*, *The Dillards Live . . . Almost*, and *Pickin' and Fiddlin'*. While playing the old favorites brings back pleasant memories, fresh new tunes keep popping into Douglas' head, and he expects to continue to evolve musically.

Albums by Douglas Dillard & the Doug Dillard Band

The Banjo Album (Together, 1968)
The Fantastic Expedition of Dillard and Clark (A&M, 1969)
Through the Morning, Through the Night (A&M, 1970)

Dueling Banjos (20th Century, 1973)
You Don't Need a Reason to Sing (20th Century, 1974)
Heaven (Flying Fish, 1976)
Glitter Grass from the Nashwood Hollyville Strings
    (Flying Fish, 1976)
Jack Rabbit (Flying Fish, 1979)
Permanent Wave (Flying Fish, 1980)
What's That (Flying Fish Records, 1986)
Heartbreak Hotel (Flying Fish Records, 1989)

Mitch Jayne

All Mitch Jayne ever wanted was a dependable type-writer, an endless supply of high quality bond paper, a fireplace large enough to heat a medieval castle, and a reliable mailman. His mind was already brimming with story ideas and, like most good humorists, he could find comedy in nearly every daily human activity.

Performing with the Dillards offered Mitch the freedom to develop his writing. The band generally played their gigs at night, and with Mitch being an early riser from his schoolteacher days, he had plenty of time to develop story ideas.

"When you play music you usually play at night, and if we needed to rehearse we would do that around 4 p.m. This meant I had most of the day to write. I'd get up by six, drag my portable typewriter by the pool, and work on whatever writing projects I had going. I generally would work on two projects at a time, sometimes three, unless I was working on a book," Mitch said.

His diligence paid off as his first book, *Forest In*

The revised Dillards: Herb Pederson (top left) helped change the musical direction of the Dillards upon the departure of Douglas Dillard.
—*photo courtesy of the Dillards*

What's that! Douglas and Homer Dillard are joined by a friend. He's a little squirrelly at times. —*photo courtesy of Douglas Dillard*

Preparing for the Newport Folk Festival. —*photo courtesy of Dean Webb*

Picking and Fiddling with Byron Berline: Ironically, although this cabin was located in California, it bears a striking resemblance to those found in the Ozark hills. The Dillards later discovered that it was built by a transplanted Missourian.
—*photo courtesy of Douglas Dillard*

Available on CD

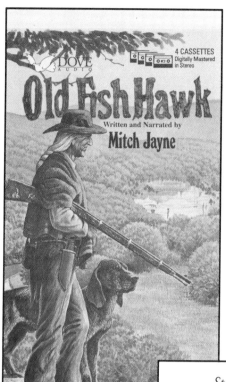

Books by Mitch Jayne
available on audio
cassette.

The Wind, was published in 1966, with *Old Fish Hawk* following in 1969. The film version of *Old Fish Hawk* was released in 1979 and is available on video.

Mitch earned a name for himself as a creative wizard during the height of the Dillards' popularity. Dick Clark met Mitch during an appearance by the Dillards on one of Clark's numerous music-oriented television programs. Clark became intrigued by Mitch's comic talents, and offered him a full-time position as a troubleshooter for his various productions. Mitch declined, as his first loyalty remained to the Dillards. Clark understood and asked Mitch to work for him whenever the Dillards' schedule permitted. Mitch agreed and worked for Clark on and off over the next two years, writing numerous television and movie treatments.

Sale of the film rights of *Old Fish Hawk* to 20th Century Fox enabled Mitch to retire from the road in 1974 at the age of 45. He and his wife Lee were in the process of finalizing their divorce, and a return to the Ozarks and a fresh start sounded promising to Mitch.

He packed up all his plunder, retreated to the Mark Twain National Forrest east of Salem, Missouri, and built a log cabin. Building the house was a massive undertaking and a labor of love. The roof alone consisted of thirty-three thousand handmade wooden shingles fashioned by friends and family members.

The fireplace was that of his dreams, large enough to heat the entire house and to roast a healthy-size-cow. Here Mitch felt at home, and at peace with himself and the world. He settled into the task of reacquainting himself with the woods, the streams, the mountains, and most importantly, the Ozark people. Mitch spent the next seven years researching book projects, writing magazine and newspaper columns, and hammering out manuscripts. Then, shortly before Christmas 1981, Mitch lost nearly everything he possessed — except his life — in the span of five terrifying minutes.

"We always kept a fire going in the house, and that night we had this incredible roaring fire going. I was getting ready to wind the clock before turning in to bed when I looked out the window and noticed that the woods were glowing. I realized in a minute that it was the house that was on fire," Mitch said. "Sparks from the chimney had ignited the roof shingles, and within five minutes the entire house was gone."

Destroyed in the fire were all of Mitch's personal records, which included two completed book manuscripts and research material, family heirlooms, his gun collection, photographs and papers from his days with the Dillards, and a typewriter used by Mark Twain, which had been given to Mitch as a gift. The loss devastated him; he took nearly five years to recover.

When the original Dillard members heard of the tragedy, they hurried to Mitch's side. The band reunited to hold a benefit concert for Mitch. Funds received in the concert went to build Mitch a new home using the previous house's foundation. The townspeople and neighbors pitched in to build the house, but though it was a wonderful act of love and kindness, Mitch still felt the pain of loss.

"The second house was built by my neighbors, and it meant a lot to me. I could tell you who put in each nail, almost, but it still wasn't that first house, which had been the house of my dreams."

Today Mitch spends his hours writing columns for six magazines, including *Bluegrass Unlimited, Bluegrass Now, Today's Farmer,* and *The Missouri Conservationist,* along with a weekly newspaper column for *The Current Wave* in Eminence, Missouri. He has written three books of humor columns: *Stories From Home, Volume 1* and *Volume 2,* both of which were produced on audiocassette by Wildstone Media of St. Louis. Mitch's most recent collection of humorous essays are contained in the book *Some More Home Grown Stories and Home Fried Lies,* published in 1994.

Wildstone Media, which purchased the rights to *Old Fish Hawk,* released an audio version of Mitch's breakthrough novel in April 1995. All of the audiobooks are narrated by the only person who can do them justice, Mitch Jayne. He is also busy at work reworking and polishing the manuscript for *The Glory Hole War,* a novel set in the fictitious Ozark village of Morning Glory, Missouri.

All of Mitch's published work is chock-full of rich mountain humor, relying on wit rather than sex, violence, or four-letter words to keep the reader's attention. Yet, included into the mix are vibrant, colorful characters whose lives reflect the wholesome small-town values, the memory of which appears to grow dimmer with each passing day. Did folks who cared for their neighbors, children, and towns actually exist, or were they only the by-product of wishful thinking?

Mitch is a master of dialogue, and demonstrates his subtle inventiveness when he decides to stand atop his soap box and orate about the self-destructive side effects of government handouts. In *The Glory Hole War*, two of the central characters are newspaper editors, giving Mitch the use of two editorial pages.

Reading the manuscript, one can visualize a little bit of Mayberry and its citizenry's values appearing in the town of Morning Glory. The following is an excerpt from *The Glory Hole War*.

> *Morning Glory, population one hundred and fifty, is a proud little town, but it wasn't pride alone that kept it from asking for things that other towns asked for, and got, from the state and federal government. Things such as new roads, bigger schools, housing for the aged, disaster loans, or grants of some kind. Morning Glory was, and is, satisfied and happy with what it has always had, because down through the years this little town has kept it's values. And I'm not too embarrassed to admit that those values are immensely sentimental; love, caring for other people, and a sense of responsibility for what the Bible calls sharing.*
>
> *When the roads needed repairing, the people of this little town got together and repaired them.*
>
> *When other towns decided to consolidate and bus their children to bigger schools, these people kept their one-room school, with the love, family ties and personal involvement that are part of it.*
>
> *When people in other towns borrowed funds from the government and built old peoples' homes and retirement centers for the aged, Morning Glory looked at it's elderly people and saw no problems. Old people were never considered to be different, and continued to belong, to be looked after by family, friends, and neighbors, and accepted as important members of the community.*
>
> *When a house burned, Morning Glory erected a new one, and man, woman, and child took pride in that act of friendship.*

Morning Glory has never had a welfare office, a sheltered workshop, or unemployment office, or any of the other agencies that government establishes to maintain the machinery of efficiency. It has no loan company, such as you must have in towns where people don't really know each other and must seek help from strangers.

Dean Webb

By the end of the 1970s, Dean was living in Kentucky while Rodney called Nashville his home. During a two-year stint with Earl Scruggs from 1979-1981, Dean and Rodney visited Silver Dollar City and Branson. Lonnie Hoppers, Dean and Rodney's old friend, invited the pair to join his show at Silver Dollar City. With the number of club dates dwindling, Dean decided to pull up stakes and returned to his Missouri roots in 1983.

Rodney and Dean performed regularly at the Gaslight Theater during the end of the 1983 season. The theater only seated five hundred tourists and the shows were always sold out, which caused bitterness among those turned away at the door. The following season the pair's show was moved to the Silver Dollar City Amphitheater, which offered ample seating.

An unwritten agreement between the two tourist spots was that Silver Dollar City would provide daytime entertainment for tourists, while Branson would offer the night life. Clubs in Branson were already starting matinee shows, so Silver Dollar City countered with an evening country music show which featured the Dillards as the show's centerpiece attraction. Dean and Rodney performed in the Silver Dollar Jubilee until 1988.

Today Dean Webb leads a quiet life in Branson, Missouri, working at the Tony Orlando Theater just to keep himself busy. His connection with the Dillards is as overseer of Stick and Stone Productions. The company offers Dillard merchandise through a mail-order catalog.

Decade Waltz, Wheatstraw Suite and *Copperfields* are among Dean's favorite albums. He admits to missing the adventures on the road and playing before live audiences.

"There is a certain thrill you get when you see that people like what you are doing. Now, if they start throwing tomatoes at you the thrill is gone. It is almost a reciprocal type thing. The more applause you receive, the better you play. Looking back at all the photographs, you can always tell when things were going right and the audiences were really enjoying your work. In those photographs you never looked better and you always look happy," Dean said.

Rodney Dillard

Starting about the time of *Wheatstraw Suite,* Rodney found himself branching out into the production end of music. Along with producing the Dillards' material, Rodney did production work for Roy Clark, Pat Boone, Keith Carradine, and his brother Douglas. As his reputation as a musical producer grew he was tabbed to produce larger projects, such as the critically acclaimed *Tribute To Woody Guthrie* album.

"There is a lot that goes into the production of an album. You try to pull the right players together

to create the right moment. The producer has to ensure that the music is going down on tape right," he
said.

Earl Scruggs, Rodney and Dean teamed up together in 1979 for an extended tour, an event which
ranks as one of Rodney's career highlights. Although the Dillards and Scruggs' paths had frequently crossed throughout their concert appearances, Rodney had never performed in public with
Scruggs. The decision to join forces came after
Scruggs attended a post-broadcast party for the par-
ticipants of a Johnny Cash television show.

"Earl came over to the hotel one night after one
of the Cash shows. All of the performers were in the
room including the band Bread, Linda Ronstadt,
Herb Pedersen, and I. We all played and sang, then a
while later Earl called and asked if I'd like to go on
tour with him. Teaming up with Earl in 1979 and
1980 was one of the neatest things I've ever done. He
is one of the most interesting people I've met,"
Rodney said.

Rodney later performed on the celebrated *Earl
Scruggs and Friends* album.

Rodney's decision to pull off the road and settle
down in Branson in 1982 was made for him by his
then nine-year-old son, Brian. At the time Rodney
was a single parent and preparing to remarry. Rodney had visited Branson during his touring days with
Scruggs. The musicians were flying over the Table
Rock Dam when Rodney noticed houses dotting the
hillside overlooking the lake and dam. Rodney turned
to Scruggs and commented that it would be great to
live on the hill overlooking the dam. Two years later,
Rodney looked down from his house and watched the

activity along the dam, only to realize that he had fulfilled his dream.

"I needed to do something. Our plan was to rent a house on the lake and spend the summer at Silver Dollar City," Rodney explained. "We thought it would give Brian a chance to form a relationship with my new wife, Beverly, and at the same time allow us to get settled into our new marriage. By summer's end I was asked to stay on as a consultant for Silver Dollar City."

For the next six years Rodney, Beverly and Dean performed together in a two-hour evening variety show held at the Silver Dollar City Amphitheater. The show featured music and comedy indigenous to the Ozarks, and was eventually featured as a special on the then Christian Broadcasting Network, later renamed The Family Channel.

Return to Mayberry served to rekindle the original Dillards' desire to perform together. The band reunited in 1989 for what would become a critically acclaimed world tour. A Los Angeles Times reviewer noted that on stage the Dillards, "still make magic with light-speed picking and three and four-part harmonies that can only have been learned on a back porch in the Ozarks. "The thirtieth anniversary of *The Andy Griffith Show* in 1990 provided another infusion of interest in the Dillards, plus Steve Cooley. Originally the group had agreed to play four concerts. The number of concert dates grew to eight, then twelve and upward, until finally the Dillards played one hundred and thirty-two dates, including performances in Great Britain and Japan.

"I tell all of our friends that Rodney left home to attend the thirtieth reunion of *The Andy Griffith Show*

The Dillard's *Let It Fly* album contained the group's first Grammy nominated song—what else—"Darlin Boys." (l-r) Rodney Dillard, Steve Cooley, Dean Webb and Mitch Jayne.
—*photo courtesy of Vanguard Records*

and wound up reunioning for three years," Beverly Dillard laughed.

Before parking the Darlings' truck for the last time, the band recorded two highly acclaimed albums on the Vanguard Records label, *Let It Fly* and *Take Me Along for the Ride. Pulse Magazine* selected *Let It Fly* as the number-two country music album of the year, behind Alan Jackson's *Here In The Real World* and outpacing offerings by Vince Gill, Carlene Carter, Dwight Yoakam, and Mary Chapin Carpenter. *Let It Fly* also saw the return of Herb Pedersen, who produced the album along with providing vocals and rhythm guitar.

Ironically, it was during this period that the Dillards recorded the song, "Darlin Boys," as a whimsical tribute to their fictitious alter egos. The song garnered the band a Grammy nomination in 1990, the band's first such distinction.

"We did "Darlin Boys" as a hoot. Isn't that always the way?" Rodney commented. "You toil away for years trying to achieve some recognition and you get nothing, but then you do something just for the simple enjoyment of doing it and you wind up with a Grammy nomination. Receiving the Grammy nomination wasn't the thrill that it would have been had it come thirty years earlier. You tend to get bigger thrills when you are young. I felt the same way when we appeared on Johnny Cash's television show, which was broadcast from the Grand Old Opry. It was nice to be able to work the Opry stage before it closed, but the rush would have been greater and the thrill would have been greater had it come earlier in our career."

A Mayberry celebration in Branson, Missouri reunited the Dillards with Howard Morris and Maggie Peterson. Beverly Dillard's friendship with Howard Morris nearly ended in premature disaster. Following the celebration, Morris stayed in Branson for a short visit, along with Maggie Peterson.

When Beverly Dillard and Maggie Peterson decided to spend an afternoon shopping, Morris asked to join the excursion. Beverly loaded up the van and was trying to close the back door when it became stuck and refused to close. Beverly slammed the door down with three successive bam, bam, bams, and could not figure out why the door would not go down. To her horror, Beverly turned and discovered

Howard Morris proudly displays a reward from the Mayberry reunion in Branson, Missouri. Ernest T. always wanted to marry into the Darling family.   —*photo courtesy of Rodney Dillard*

that she had been slugging Morris on the head with the van door. Morris was stunned by the repeated blows and looked as though he was going to pass out. Fortunately, he was not seriously injured.

"Today whenever something like that happens we call it pulling a Howie," Beverly said.

Morris survived and left Branson with a unique treasure—a velvet portrait of Elvis Presley.

Seeing Morris and Peterson was like old times, Rodney said.

"I believe Maggie gets prettier each year," Rodney contends. "She was a pretty girl on the Griffith show, but she is even prettier today."

Today Maggie Peterson is Maggie Peterson-Mancuso. She married musician Gus Mancuso, fifteen years ago, and the couple live quietly in Las Vegas. They tend their garden in the summer and have been known at times to keep a few chickens.

For the past seven years the former Charlene Darling Wash has worked for the Nevada Film Commission. She recently finished an eight-month stint as a location coordinator on the Martin Scorsese film *Casino*, which stars Sharon Stone and Robert DiNero and is set in the Las Vegas of the 1970s.

Ironically, Maggie found herself in the celebrity role when word of her dual identity reached the cast and crew. Suddenly, she was the one signing autographs and being the object of photographers. A similar incident occurred at Caesar's Palace, when Vince Gill and his band became aware of Charlene Darling's presence. Within a matter of seconds the roles had reversed, and Maggie Peterson was star of the moment.

When asked to describe the Dillards, Maggie Peterson replied, "They are all so kind and just—darlings."

Rodney's growing association with the Branson music scene was one of two events which led to the end of the Dillards Reunion Tour in 1991. Jim Stafford, well entrenched in the Branson entertainment business, offered Rodney the position of Vice President of Creative Productions. More importantly, Beverly and Rodney were expecting the arrival of a baby girl, Rachel Dillard.

"When we started the tour we all agreed that we would perform until everyone got tired of performing. The Dillards probably would have continued to work occasionally had I not committed to Stafford. His show ran seven days a week, and I performed in the show. Beverly was pregnant, and I wanted to be home with her and Rachel when Rachel arrived," Rodney said. "Working in Branson meant I was only five minutes from the theater, and the road no longer held the appeal for me that it had in my youth. Traveling on the road with the Dillards again was a lot of fun, because we were able to see a lot of old friends that we hadn't seen in years, but after a while the tour became a grind."

Rodney Dillard serves as Production Executive for a subsidary Patch Entertainment, operating out of Branson. Patch Entertainment operates several magazines, including *Computer Shoppers Weekly, Soccer,* and *Shutterbug.* Patch's broad interest also comprises an entertainment division which includes a television production company, a television station, and a recording studio. On January 4th, 1995, Patch Entertainment acquired Caravell Studio in Branson, where Rodney's duties include production coordinator, studio manager, and studio overseer for Patch, along with working in artist development.

Today Rodney claims to have nothing to say musically. His interest is in guiding others through the minefields which he encountered in his journey. However, Rodney acknowledges that his attitude may change in another few years if he enters another period of growth.

When asked if he is bitter that groups such as the Eagles and Crosby, Stills and Nash were able to garner more commercial success than the Dillards, Rodney maintains that he is content with the Dillards' musical accomplishments.

"We made a certain mark on the musical process. The Dillards weren't the comet like the Eagles, but we are a star in the star field. What the Dillards did was totally out of ignorance. It was a bunch of young guys that said, 'Let's go over and see what is over that next hill or that next ridge.' I felt trapped as a young kid, because I didn't know what was over that next ridge. Believe me, I've been over a lot of ridges," Rodney offered.

Ozark Nights

*"We were the best of friends on the porch back
    then
We were next of kin to the mandolin
And Orion in the Milky Way, laughed at what
    we found
And the Dipper high in Missouri skies, stopped
    and listened to the sound
While Doug and Dean and Mitch and me, like
    wild geese taking flight
Born on wings of banjo strings, on a warm dark
    Ozark night"*
                    —(Jim Ratts - Ozark Nights)

John McEuen's closest brush with a mystical experience came in 1964, when a friend invited the teenager
to catch a show at the Paradox Club in Orange County, California. The hot band appearing in the club
was the Dillards. McEuen had never heard of the
group, and was skeptical. Not knowing what to expect but trusting his friend, McEuen sat patiently in
the audience and waited for something to happen.
He didn't have to wait long.

"When Doug Dillard came out and kicked off
with "Hickory Hollow," I don't think I took a breath
for awhile. I had never seen a performance, or had
heard music, that excited me like the Dillards,"
McEuen recalled.

Mitch recalls spotting McEuen in the audience

one night holding a banjo. "We played so many clubs where there would be some big teen-age kid on the front row whose face, the first time he heard that five-string banjo cooking, would light up and glow like a Christmas tree. John McEuen is a perfect example. He used to sit on the front row at The Mecca and watch Douglas intently. He would bring his banjo to the club and keep it in his lap. He did that so he could watch Douglas' fingers and try to imitate him right then and there. The first time I spotted him in the audience with his banjo I thought, 'that yokel is going to play along with us,' but he had enough sense not to do that."

The night at the Paradox Club altered McEuen's musical life. Never one of those toe-tapping listeners, McEuen discovered himself doing that during the Dillards' performance. For the next two years, he caught an average of two Dillards' shows a week whenever the group was in the Los Angeles area. He bought all their albums, studied their style, and visited the group backstage frequently until they all became friends. When McEuen later helped form the Nitty Gritty Dirt Band, the musical influences of the Dillards carried over into the Dirt Band's style.

Twenty-five years after their first encounter, Rodney Dillard and McEuen started chatting about the Dillards reunion tour. McEuen asked Rodney if he could have four days of the Dillards' time to make an attempt at capturing the spirit and raw energy of the Dillards on film.

"I wanted to capture the excitement of what their music was like to me. The basic premise of the film is that the Dillards are practicing inside an old farmhouse and I sneak in and watch them play, which al-

Shooting a scene from *A Night In The Ozarks*, a video
of the Dillards by John McEuen.
—*photo courtesy of Keith Case and Assoc.*

lows their music to be caught up close," McEuen explained.

The project became a labor of love for McEuen,
and fellow friends and fans of the Dillards. Scott
Flanagan helped finance the film, which brought in

an ensemble of highly skilled and talented lighting, camera, and sound crew members. The concert was recorded with five cameras over five days.

A majority of the film footage was shot both inside and outside a vacant home belonging to Missouri State Representative Ken Feibleman. Friends of the Dillards decorated the house with antiques and memorabilia, giving it the appearance that travelers have stopped at the home of the Dillards' proud parents.

At times the sweet harmonic voices of the Dillards are backed by an unseen choir of cicadas and crickets, outnumbering their Mormon Tabernacle counterparts by a hundredfold. This is a fitting reminder of the Dillards' humble origins, singing and laughing on the back porch of Mitch Jayne's home nearly three decades earlier.

"Watching and hearing Rodney sing "The Old Home Place" and "I'll Never See My Home Again" left me just as excited as I was when I first heard them," McEuen said.

Adding Homer Dillard to the line-up was a suggestion offered by Rodney which proved to be a brilliant stroke, as the Dillards' father nearly stole the show at times with his fiddling and dancing.

The video *A Night in the Ozarks* was released in 1989 on the Audiolithograph Society label. The eighty-minute video features nineteen songs including "Ebo Walker," "Doug's Tune," "Banjo in the Hollow" and "Dooley."

Since its initial release to the home video market the film has aired repeatedly on the Americana Network, a fitting location for a band whose roots are pure American.

Mitch*

Douglas**

Rodney*

Dean*

*photo courtesy of the Dillards
**photo courtesy of Penny Clapp

McEuen takes tremendous pride in the final product as the film continues to introduce the Dillards and their music to new audiences. "The Dillards are an American treasure which has never been fully discovered," McEuen asserts. *A Night in the Ozarks* remains available through the Audiolithograph Society, PO Box 4203, Palace Verdes Peninsula, California, 90274. Orders can also be placed by calling the toll free number: 1-800-722-7855. The cost of the video is $19.95 plus shipping and handling.

Fans of the Dillards can also purchase videos, cassettes, and compact discs, along with Dillard T-shirts, photographs, and caps, through Stick and Stone Productions. For an up-to-date listing of available merchandise write to Stick and Stone Productions PO Box 351, Kimberling City, Missouri, 65686.

Fans of Mitch Jayne's Ozark humor can check out audio tapes produced and distributed by Wildstone Audio, PO Box 511580, St. Louis, Missouri, 63151. The books on tape, *Old Fish Hawk* and *Stories From Home,* are narrated by Mitch. His latest offering, *More Home Grown Stories and Home Fried Lies,* is available at $6.50 per copy directly from Mitch Jayne, 105 Aldeah Avenue, Columbia, Missouri, 65203.

ORDER FORM

Use this form to order additional copies of
Everybody on the Truck!
for your friends or family members.

Name: _____

Address: _____

City: _____ St:____ Zip: _____

Daytime phone: (_____)_____

    If gift, message that you would like enclosed: _____

_____

_____

_____

    If gift, ship to:

    Name _____

    Address: _____

    City: _____ St:____ Zip: _____

Method of Payment: *(Make payable to **Eggman Publishing, Inc.**)*
    ❑ Check   ❑ Money Order   ❑ VISA   ❑ MasterCard   ❑ Discover

Card# _____ Exp. _____

Signature: _____
       Required for credit card purchases

Quantity: _____ x $12.95 =	$_____
Shipping & Handling Quantity: _____ x $ 1.00 =	$_____
Sub Total:	$_____
TN residents add 8.25% sales tax	$_____
Total:	$_____

Please return form and payment to: **Eggman Publishing, Inc.**
                                  2909 Poston Avenue Ste 203
                                  Nashville, TN 37203

FOR FASTER SERVICE CALL 1-800-409-7277

Thank You!
Your order will be shipped within 1-3 weeks from receipt